3.1.Λ

AFTER THE WAKE
An essay on the contemporary avant-garde

Christopher Butler

CLARENDON PRESS · OXFORD
1980

Oxford University Press, Walton Street Oxford OX2 6DP

OXFORD   LONDON   GLASGOW

NEW YORK   TORONTO   MELBOURNE   WELLINGTON

KUALA LUMPUR   SINGAPORE   JAKARTA   HONG KONG   TOKYO

DELHI   BOMBAY   CALCUTTA   MADRAS   KARACHI

NAIROBI   DAR ES SALAAM   CAPE TOWN

Published in the United States
by Oxford University Press, New York

British Library Cataloguing in Publication Data
Butler, Christopher
  After the wake.
  1. Arts, Modern – 20th century
  I. Title
  700'.9'04   NX456   79–41663

  ISBN 0–19–815766–5

Phototypeset in V.I.P. Baskerville by
Western Printing Services Ltd, Bristol
Printed by Butler and Tanner Ltd, Frome.

213934

CONTENTS

LIST OF PLATES

INTRODUCTION

The essay which follows is concerned with some of the avant-garde literature, painting, and music produced since the publication of *Finnegans Wake*. Writing about contemporary art is pleasurable, but also risky; one deals with a world without any conventionally agreed order. It is not given to us as the product of some academic consensus, an ordered series of Eliotic monuments sanctified by time and tended by critics. No such landscape is well established in anyone's mind yet, and even if we think we know (as we usually do) who the major figures might be, we are less sure of what to do about them. What follows is truly an essay, on an artistic scene whose structure at times seems to owe far more to the 'happening' than to any easily discernible historical or logical order.

For most of us, even those whose good intentions are backed up by an awareness of the art of the modernist period, find the contemporary situation very confusing. The basic reason for this may well be that avant-garde art does not yet communicate very directly (or even pleasurably) with the public at large. This seems to offer a golden opportunity to the critic, who can indulge his liberal and pacific instincts by interposing himself between the embattled artist and his bewildered audience, and beginning to explain. But this is, I think, much too optimistic a view. The gap originally opened by the modernists between advanced art and the audience of reasonable men and women of goodwill is far too wide for there to be any easy critical solutions or easy critical guides to the contemporary situation.

My plan has been to argue that in the 1950s radically new conventions for the language of art were developed by writers, musicians, and painters who wished to break away from modernism. I then go on to give an exposition, following so far as is possible the artists' own statements of intention, of some major works of this 'postmodern' period, in which I discern a contrast between those which are dominated by a theory of their own rule-dominated means of creation, and those whose method is antithetical to this, being irrationalist, indeterminate, or aleatory. I then use this corpus of examples (and others) to consider more generally the nature of the avant-garde and the cultural context which makes it possible, and to analyse critically in conclusion the nature of the 'aesthetic experience' which it offers. My main aim is to show that there are common, though not necessarily explicit, aesthetic principles underlying much recent art. It is at this level that the close analogies between the arts can be appreciated and an implied *Zeitgeist* discerned. These 'agreements in principle', as fragile as any in the political sphere, help us to build up a picture, admittedly a provisional one, of the way in which contemporary art functions within our culture. This is not to suggest that I attempt any great philosophical rigour in what follows, nor, if my mere introduction may be allowed to attempt to disarm criticism, have I tried to be scholarly or comprehensive. I have concentrated on a few obviously major figures, and upon a limited selection of their works. Thus the musicians chiefly discussed are Messiaen, Cage, Boulez, Stockhausen, and Berio. I realize that this involves some injustice; and if time and space had allowed I would have looked equally closely at the work of Maxwell Davies, Ligeti, Lutoslawski, Penderecki, and Henze. Similar omissions will no doubt be noticed for the other arts.

There are a number of great works in this period, but they have been produced within an excessively fast-evolving cultural environment, deliberately strewn at times with trivial rubbish, and at others with impossibly complex mazes liberally supplied by their creators with deadends. Our understanding is thus hedged about with almost impossible challenges and deliberately offered frustrations; hence the occasionally rather Manichaean cast of my argument. And yet a period in which we have had Messiaen, Beckett, and Pollock at work does not lack great artists, and their distinction and originality make it unnecessary to fall into a very common critical trap: that in which the critic, trying to make sense of the contemporary, falls prone to a nostalgia for an earlier order, in particular for the modernist achievement.

Of course there is a problem here, both of influence and of ultimate independence. But I have tried to show in what follows that postmodern art requires a quite distinct reorientation of our critical and psychological responses, and that although much contemporary art may hint very strongly at its modernist origins, the mere searching out of historical parallels will do surprisingly little to aid our understanding, and may inhibit us from realizing that it reflects a quite distinct phase of historical development. Butor's *Mobile* (1962) is thus as far removed in time from *Ulysses* (1922) as the latter is from Maupassant's *Une vie* of 1882, and they all three reflect quite different assumptions concerning the relationship of the act of writing to experience.

Nevertheless the first demand of the work of art is that it be appraised not as a historical symptom but on its own terms. It may prove to be self-explanatory or it may not; if not, of course one may look backwards for help, but causal historical explanations alone will never make critical assessments. What is ultimately up for judgement is the experience which the art contemporary with our own life history may provide for us.

PART ONE: HISTORY

Men wiser and more learned than I have discerned in history a plot, a rhythm, a predetermined pattern. These harmonies are concealed from me. I can see only one emergency following upon another.
H.A.L. Fisher.

All past consciousness is bunk. History is bunk. Like Henry Ford said about technology—there is nothing to be learned from history any more. We're in science fiction now.
Allen Ginsberg.

Chapter One: Postmodernism and Innovation

I

There are, unfortunately, no tidily demarcated historical periods. Although all the artists whom I shall call 'postmodern' consolidate their work and reputations after 1945, their roots in many cases go back into the Modernist period; and conversely, many great modernists (Picasso, Stravinsky, Auden, Stevens, Carlos Williams, Mirò, Chagall, Britten, and Shostakovitch) worked well on into the postwar period. Such biographical facts will not much help us to define postmodernism in any case. If we wish to characterize a period of artistic rather than political history, our concern had much better be with the changing sense of tradition within it, its attempts to break away from the past, and with the evolution of new, but common and characteristic aesthetic assumptions. For the arts change, not simply when men die, but by adopting new frameworks and modifying their own languages. The process is very like that which Thomas Kuhn has described for change and revolution in science; we move from groups doing what is 'normal' for their period to the establishment of breakaway groups forming round men or women who have managed to make some radical conceptual or theoretical leap. It is often only with hindsight that we realize that things have changed, for example when we notice that a critic is willing to assert that 'Today *Bouvard and Pécuchet* seems more subversive than *Ulysses*.'[1] If he is right, then the old order of Modernism has changed indeed.

It is in fact the point of transition between the two periods, the moment when new models of artistic activity begin to function within the tradition, that is most difficult to locate. But upon its location may turn a vital question: is postmodernism a mere, possibly decadent, development of modernism, or did it fight through to a real independence? My argument will affirm the latter proposition; and the beginnings of its proof might be attempted if I give a very brief historical sketch.

Firstly, there seem to be, as one might expect, works which mediate between the two periods, since they are both the products of modernism and major influences in the post-war period. If we take literature as a representative example (leaving the transitions in painting and music for later) I would suggest that *Finnegans Wake*, *La Nausée*, and the *Cantos* have this kind of status. The reasons for this assertion should become amply clear in what follows but, briefly stated, they would be the huge overload of information provided by the multiple-structured language of Joyce's *Wake* (a supreme example of self-conscious 'écriture') which is awesomely prophetic of the demands made on the reader (or indeed hearer and viewer) by many postmodern works of art. For *Finnegans Wake* is a recognized predecessor of those later works which are about the process of writing itself, and which have so profoundly disturbed our received notions concerning 'realism'.[2] Sartre's *La Nausée*, although it moves to a typically modernist (indeed Proustian) conclusion, in which the protagonist's epiphany leads to his decision to redeem his experience in art, is also a key work, not only for its existentialism and its obsession with things, but also for its pivotal position in that series of novels from Proust to Robbe-Grillet and beyond, which progressively subordinate the nineteenth-century liberal independence of character to the phenomenological twists and turns of the narrator's own reflective consciousness. (Thus Camus echoes Sartre's hero Roquentin, in his *Le Mythe de Sisyphe*: 'Dans cet univers, l'œuvre est alors la chance unique de maintenir sa conscience et d'en fixer les aventures. Créer, c'est vivre deux fois.')[3]

The influence of Pound has been well documented.[4] The main point to stress here is that his looseness of construction in the *Cantos*, his colloquiality, and the irrational, collaged effect of his use of sources, have inspired many subsequent poets. Most notably, Carlos Williams's *Paterson*, whose first book was published in 1946 and encouraged a decisive shift of interest amongst poets, like Olson, Dorn, Creeley, and Duncan, towards the methods of Pound rather than those of Eliot. Robert Lowell indeed hailed this book as a 'sort of anti-*Cantos* rooted in America'[5] and sustained his early enthusiasm in an article written fifteen years later: 'Williams is part of the great breath of our culture. *Paterson* is our *Leaves of Grass*. The times have changed. A drastic experimental art is now expected and demanded.'[6] Thus Eliot's deadening critical authoritarianism and schoolmasterly fixing of the syllabus was to some degree cast aside (along with his essentially conservative return to a Symbolist aesthetic in *Four Quartets*). Lowell himself reflects this change in his move from a highly wrought and densely symbolic early style through *Life Studies* to the essentially intuitive, non-narrative movement of *Notebook*.[7] This reaction against order is, as we shall see, a key development in postmodernism, and was picked up very quickly by Lowell's friend Randall Jarrell. Noting the resemblance of *Paterson* to the middle and later *Cantos*, he suggests that 'the organisation of irrelevance (or, perhaps the irrelevance of organisation) suggests itself as a name for this category of structure'.[8]

Indeed, the dialectic between the huge over-organization of *Finnegans Wake* and the deliberate lack of it in the *Cantos* conditions the whole of the postmodern period; and what mediates between these at all points is the phenomenological concentration upon the mental processes of the artist, as prefigured in *La Nausée*. The present structuralist insistence upon the play of language, the manipulation of codes by the artist, is in many ways an extension of this interest in the dynamics of the creative process.

Artists have of course always been thought of as 'free' in the modernist, supposedly anti-bourgeois, experimentalist sense. This freedom was greatly reinforced by the growth and influence of existentialism in this transitional period. The literary works of the existentialists were largely conservative in technique, and will not be considered in what follows. But their underlying philosophy not only underwrote the artist's independent creation of value (thus influencing even the action painters of New York), but also offered a point of departure for the *nouveau roman*. Thus Robbe-Grillet's notorious 'chosisme' is largely a reaction against a Sartrean complicity, even if a nauseous one, with objects in the external world, and the 'aventure' which we are supposed to enjoy in the twists and turns of the new novelist's 'écriture' must owe a great deal to Antoine Roquentin's insight:

> Voici ce que j'ai pensé: pour que l'événement le plus banal devienne une aventure, il faut et il suffit qu'on se mette à le *raconter*. C'est ce qui dupe les gens; un homme, c'est toujours un conteur d'histoires, il vit entouré de ses histoires et des histoires d'autrui, il voit tout à travers elles; et il cherche à vivre comme s'il la racontait. Mais il faut choisir: vivre ou raconter.[9]

Sartre is of course open to the accusation of having defied his own insight by writing this last sentence, of having written a work which was essentially realist, even 'bourgeois' in so far as its philosophical aim was to show how the world held together in a necessary way, undeconstructed by man's story-telling urge, which is the key to that 'arbitrariness of the sign' of which we have since heard so much. Nevertheless, it seems that Sartre and the new novelists are at one in seeing the act of writing as a means of redeeming experience. Thus the resolution of the protagonist of Michel Butor's *La Modification* (1957) to write a book owes everything to Antoine Roquentin's example. He has travelled by train from Paris to Rome, and in a long meditation decided not to continue an extra-marital affair. The train stops: and in the concluding words of the novel the Sartrean word 'aventure' has a crucial position:

> Vous entendez les cris des porteurs, les sifflets, les halètements, les crissements des autres trains.
> Vous vous levez, remettez votre manteau, prenez votre valise, ramassez votre livre.
> Le mieux, sans doute, serait de conserver à ces deux villes leurs relations géographiques réelles,
> et de tenter de faire revivre sur le mode de la lecture cette épisode crucial de votre aventure, le mouvement qui s'est produit dans votre esprit accompagnant le déplacement de votre corps d'une gare à l'autre à travers tous les paysages intermédiaires.
> vers ce livre futur et nécessaire dont vous tenez la forme dans votre main.
> Le couloir est vide. Vous regardez la foule sur le quai. Vous quittez le compartiment.[10]

There is of course a more general influence of existentialism in this transitional period: and it is a moral one. It
provided a sense of purpose which was necessary for recov-
ery from the fascist period, and gave confidence to the
avant-garde. Its long-term effects, however, seem to me to
belong more to the history of liberalism than to experimental
art. The moral assumptions of existentialism did indeed
underlie the principles of much 'avant-garde' psychiatry in
our period (in Rollo May or R.D. Laing) but they come
through most clearly in liberal novel writing. *Herzog*, *My Life
as a Man*, *Portnoy's Complaint*, *Something Happened*, let alone
Mailer's *American Dream* and 'White Negro' hipsterism, can,
it seems to me, be best understood as peculiarly existentialist
forms of confession, and the same applies to much of the
work of Berryman and Lowell. Indeed the individual's independent, often anti-ideological search for value, and the
price he pays for it in anxiety, underlie far more than the
artistic work of the post-war period. To parody Edward VII,
'We are all existentialists now.'

The third point I wish to make is much more narrowly
historical. It is that there is a confirmation of a new 'postmodern' artistic epoch in the 1950s. The examples which
follow are fairly arbitrary, but they seem to me to be ample
evidence of a new era. Ionesco and Beckett rise to prominence. The post-1945 rediscovery of the Second Viennese
School and particularly of Webern is well under way, in the
critical work of René Leibowitz, and the teaching of
Messiaen, and the music of Nono, Boulez, Henze, and
Stockhausen. Abstract expressionism as a style, and the
consequent independence of American painting, is accepted.
Round about 1959, Chabrol, Truffaut, Godard, Rivette, and
Resnais all make their first feature films, and the novels in
the mode of the *nouveau roman* already make an impressive
list: *Les Gommes* and *Martereau* in 1953, *Passage de Milan* in
1954, and *Le Voyeur* in 1955 were succeeded by many more.
In London, in 1956, the 'This is Tomorrow' exhibition at the
Whitechapel Gallery marked the beginnings of Pop art.

There is now no going back. For better or worse, this is the
age of Beckett and Robbe-Grillet, of Cage, Messiaen,

Boulez, and Stockhausen, of Pollock, Rothko, Stella, and Rauschenberg. Their work is central to what follows.

II

These historical facts all point to a great efflorescence of avant-garde activity, but one has to remember that it took place in the light of history. Thus all those artists who wished for progressive innovation in the arts after the war faced a common problem, all too easily resumed in the cant phrase 'the anxiety of influence'. For who would not be daunted by the past heroic age of modernism? In literature alone, there were Joyce, Eliot, Pound, Rilke, Yeats, Kafka, Mann, Proust, Valéry, Gide, Conrad, Lawrence, Woolf, and Faulkner to contend with, not only as influences upon creation, but also as a group which, like similar groups of painters and musicians, had dictated the *critical* response to contemporary art.

One way of dealing with the problem was to attempt to reject that past. The slogan on the third issue of the *Dada* magazine way back in 1918—'Je ne veux pas savoir s'il y a eu des hommes avant moi' ('I do not wish to know whether there were any men before me'), (Descartes)—finds a frequent echo in the postmodern period. John Cage, for example, who had introduced chance-dominated methods into musical composition, bravely assumed that he had thus brought about an irreversible change in his audience's expectations, in proclaiming that 'we will certainly listen to this other music—this totally determined music or Beethoven, or whatever, but we'll never again take it seriously'.[11] This is a heroic attitude which is happily not for most of us. Pierre Boulez also, who was mostly concerned with a radical extension of Schoenbergian atonalism, takes a very similar attitude to Cage, but with more confidence in (his own) artistic expansion rather than in critical exclusion, when he asserts that 'Les civilisations fortes et en pleine expansion sont sans mémoire, c'est à dire qu'elles rejettent, qu'elles oublient . . . L'histoire étant liquidée, on n'a plus à penser qu'à soi-même.'[12] For Boulez, the artist stands alone as the sole source of authority for his own works, and as we shall see, he indeed brought the language of music to a previously unencountered level of technical complexity. Having done this to his own satisfaction, Boulez could make the parricidal proclamation, 'Schoenberg is Dead'.[13]

Cage thus rejects the past by seeing it as ideologically unsound, and Boulez pretends to supersede it by pseudo-scientific advance; but there was yet another way out. One could simplify and start again in childlike innocence. We find this willed regression in the representative case of Frank Judd. The forms of his work are of the most basic kind; for instance in his series of six galvanized steel boxes, 40″ by 40″ by 40″, which were fixed at regular intervals to the gallery wall. When asked why he used boxes in this way, he replied that he 'wanted to get rid of any compositional effect, and the obvious way to do it is to be symmetrical'. And his hostility to what he calls 'compositional effect' is very simply explained: 'Well, those effects tend to carry with them all the structure, values, feelings, of the whole European tradition. It suits me fine if that's all down the drain.'[14]

But a complete rejection of tradition is in fact impossible, and it certainly does not guarantee the 'originality' it some-times seeks to promote. (Thus Judd, when asked if his work was not rather like that of the Bauhaus, rather disingenu-ously replied that he considered 'the Bauhaus too long ago to think about, and I never thought about it much'.)[15] We always and inevitably see the new in the light of the old, whether the artist cared to know about it or not, and such knowledge once acquired cannot simply be expunged by artist's fiat. There is always this asymmetry between the defensive exclusiveness of concern of the creative artist, and the more liberal interests of his public and critics.

It is thus possible for the latter to trace fairly clear evolutionary lines of influence for all the arts in the post-modern period. These can be of great use in familiarizing ourselves with the new. Thus there is a line from Debussy through Varèse to Cage, and from Schoenberg through Webern, Messiaen, and Boulez to Stockhausen. Our sense of this continuity can preserve us from having to treat the new work as somehow totally unexpected: and the art of the greatest composers in our period depends upon this sort of compromise between tradition and originality. In listening to Messiaen's *Quatuor pour la fin du temps* (1941) for clarinet, violin, cello, and piano, we are immediately in a refined and exalted sound world not far removed from that of Debussy's late chamber sonatas, despite the innovatory use of birdsong as melodic material, and the modal and rhythmic complications of the work, which are derived from Indian music. The latter feature is important, in so far as the 'end of time' in the work's title refers not simply to the Apocalypse (10: 5–6) but also expresses Messiaen's desire for the end of traditional musical time, based as it was upon the equal durational divisions of classical music. As we shall see later, this suspension of normal time, either through very slow tempo and sustained sounds (as in movements five and eight here) or through the use of irregular rhythms independent of the bar lines, which prevent our perception of any regular pulse, is a key feature of many postmodern works. In many cases, as here, there is a deliberate affinity with oriental music, though Messiaen himself was surprised to note that the dissociation of the rhythm and melody in the *Quatuor* is 'in the manner of Guillaume de Machaut whose work I did not know at the time'.[16] The new is thus beautifully balanced against the old in this very accessible work, whose circumstances of composition (in a German concentration camp, for the instruments which were available) are so extraordinary.

III

The arts can of course be *made* to evolve, (though not necessarily in any necessary way) by a wilful pedagogical intervention, and it is this type of attempt to overthrow or recast old traditions and styles that we come across again and again in the history of the avant-garde. This distinction, between the evolution we saw in the Messiaen example and deliberate intervention, seems to me to be a crucial one. Thus if we look to the modernist period, we might argue (very crudely and briefly) that cubism, as it developed out of Cézanne through Braque and Picasso, shows a clear line of development, each painting a modification of its predecessors, with no sudden decision to paint in a radically new style. On the other hand, the development of atonal music in the same period seems to have been much more wilful and theoretical, largely because of the sternly expressed and ruthlessly maintained authority of Schoenberg.

One might of course feel that this atonalism was purely evolutionary, an inevitable progression from the extreme chromaticism of the late nineteenth century. After all, Schoenberg's own work, particularly *Pelléas and Mélisande* and *Verklärte Nacht*, showed just how far that could go. The twelve-note scale is itself indeed a chromatic scale. But was the development of a twelve-note *system of composition* evolutionary, or the result of essentially theoretical considerations? Despite the tentativeness of Schoenberg's own explorations, this development does seem to have had the character of a severe pedagogical intervention within the historical development of music (much reinforced by Schoenberg's remarkable grip upon Berg and Webern) for which I can think of no modernist parallel in the other arts. The 'emancipation of the dissonance' was achieved by revolutionary means.

However this may be, it is certain that the systematizing example of Schoenberg, and the close study of the works of Webern in particular, encouraged composers in the post-war period to evolve methods of composition which would predetermine so far as possible the course of their own compositions. This development subserved an end of which Schoenberg would hardly have approved. This was the abolition of the composer's knowledge of the past. For in so far as he subjected himself to 'objective' rule-governed methods, he would not in principle be prey to subjective memory, to the temptation to reproduce the familiar patterns of earlier music. (Thus, as we shall see, was 'integral serialism' born.)

Thus for many composers in the 1950s, every element of musical structure, rhythm, dynamics, theme, or series, was open to radical reappraisal. Furthermore, to accept this theoretical influence was *ipso facto* to refuse to build upon the later works of Bartok, Hindemith, and Stravinsky, which were also becoming better known in the post-war years. Serialists thus cut themselves off from the (apparent) mainstream as did the Second Viennese School before them, and no immediate reconciliation between their methods and tonal ones seemed possible.

There was no longer then, within the avant-garde, any shared language for music, any complex of expectations which the composer could rely upon finding in his audience and which would correspond to what he himself had built into his structure. Tonal language, as we know, still works; what was unclear then, and remains so, is whether any other language could be made to do so. Musical expression became rather like that of *Finnegans Wake*; even though the elements (pitch, instrumentation) may have remained conventional for the time being, their organizing principles were often idiosyncratic and obscure.

Consider as a clear example of this restructuring of musical language, an early Webernian 'pointilliste' composition by Stockhausen: *Kontra-Punkte* (1952–3) for ten instruments. The preface to the score is brutally clear concerning the musical conventions which have, so to speak, been *subtracted* from the work:

no repetition, no variation, no development, no contrast. All these presuppose 'figures'—themes, motives, objects—which are repeated, varied, developed and contrasted; dissected, manipulated, magnified, reduced, modulated, transposed, mirrored or retrograded. All that has been given up since the first 'point' works. Our world—our language—our grammar.

This is a key statement concerning postmodern music, whose consequences we shall have to look at in some detail. But the result for the listener of all these renunciations of earlier compositional procedures can be briefly described. As one listens to *Kontra-Punkte*, one hears a number of isolated sounds (conventional in timbre and pitch), and one cannot use one's memory of earlier music (of conventional figuration) to create any pattern of relationships between them. There are contrasts, but they tend in the long run to cancel one another out, so that what one is most aware of is the density, the number of sounds that are there, particularly towards the end, as the instruments are discarded one by one, Haydn-fashion, to leave only the piano. It is thus texture, rather than thematic variation or any harmonic system of tensions, that is the chief feature. As Stockhausen's statement implies, there is no theme, or quasi-narrative development of theme to provide a thread of interest. Stockhausen is clear about giving this up too:

We've gone through almost two centuries of background and foreground technique—the motive, the theme, and something farther removed that is together with it. And that's why starting with *Kontra-Punkte* in 1951, I stopped dealing with that problem. I didn't want any background any more, but everything was now of equal importance.[17]

Any notion of before and after that we may have is further drastically attenuated by the work's fragmented and non-repetitive rhythms. This is a pretty radical subtraction from a time-based art; and yet the result is far from simple, for the equal importance of every unique, not to be repeated event in the music contributes to that over-loading effect which I discussed earlier.

The example I have briefly cited from Stockhausen shows how avant-garde progress of a kind could be assured by inventing new rules for the syntax and grammar of music. But problems were thereby created for the listener, because the composer's self-imposed conventions were allowed to vary so radically from work to work. In all the excitement of new discovery, there was less of an attempt than there had been amongst the Second Viennese School to agree upon assimilable conventions. The comparison I am making here with a language is of course only an analogy, but a useful one, in that we can see fairly clearly that any equally radical experimentation with a *natural* language, with its conventions of reference, and its tendency to articulate accessible worlds like our own, would not only be far more difficult to carry through, but would be very likely to result in unintelligible nonsense. (And if one believed, as some do, that tonality is equally 'natural' for music, one might well be forced to assert the same consequence.)

Nevertheless, Robbe-Grillet asserted, in 1959, that 'mon style est plus proche de la musique dodécaphonique, basée sur une série de douze sons, que de la musique tonale'.[18]

This is a nice gesture on Robbe-Grillet's part, and indicates some degree of interaction amongst avant-garde artists, in the post-war period. What it points to, I think, are the authorially imposed combinatorial aspects of his style, which are essentially counter-realistic. (They follow in many ways the crazy series and exhaustively logical enumeration of possibilities in Beckett, for example in *Watt*.) It also points, more importantly, to the fact that once again a previous background convention is being thrust away: that of a narrative whose causal relationships are like those of the 'real world'. Robbe-Grillet attacks such a notion, precisely because of its security and familiarity, its air of making the novel 'quelquonque histoire vécue': 'Bien raconter, c'est donc faire ressembler ce que l'on écrit aux schémas préfabriqués dont les gens ont l'habitude, c'est à dire à l'idée toute faite qu'ils ont de la réalité.'[19] Any such reliance upon past habits of reading and writing, (tied as they are for Robbe-Grillet to the bourgeois order) is once more to be renounced, in favour of free invention and that phenomenological investigation of the artist's own processes to which we alluded earlier: 'à tel point même, que l'invention, l'imagination, deviennent à la limite le sujet du livre.'[20] After all, says Robbe-Grillet, the armature of the anecdote had already been weakened by modernism, and story-telling of a traditional kind is now impossible, so that even if, as he admits, his own novels, *Les Gommes* and *Le Voyeur*, 'comportent . . . une "action" des plus facilement discernables . . . le mouvement de l'écriture y est plus important que celui des crimes et des passions.'[21] The autonomy of the work in relation to its own method has once again to be bought at the cost of breaking a traditional agreement between artist and audience. Not without a certain amount of fuss however; for critic still attacks critic for daring to find a narrative in Robbe-Grillet's work, and thus failing to see that everything is supposed to be given in the composition of the text, the play of its writing.[22] Thus, using the very Sartrean word 'aventure' Robbe-Grillet asserts that 'L'aventure dans mes romans peut être l'aventure d'une écriture' ('The adventure in my novels can be the adventure of writing').[23] How this is achieved is well described by Gérard Genette, and the analogy to twelve-note or serial procedures is a close one. He points out the obvious fact about many 'new novels'—that we expect scene to succeed scene in temporal succession, (to imply connectives like 'meanwhile' and 'then') but what we get, is the *same* scene modified, or an analogous scene: 'Autrement dit, il étale horizontalement, dans la continuité spatio-temporelle, la relation verticale qui unit les diverses variantes d'un thème, il dispose en série les termes d'un choix, il transpose une *concurrence* en *concaténation*.'[24]

A fuller analysis of Robbe-Grillet's methods will be given later—but I wish to emphasize here that his innovations, like those of Stockhausen, were also a means to confront earlier traditions—in this rather peculiar case, those of nineteenth-century Balzacian narrative as well as of modernism. One of his aims is to situate his own work as antagonist within that tradition, to argue that it is a repudiation of bourgeois literature, along with all the social assumptions that it implied. But this very self-conscious placing of himself has a (literally) critical sting in the tail, which will be our theme in the following chapter:

Après *Les Faux-Monnayeurs*, après Joyce, après *La Nausée*, il semble que l'on s'achemine de plus en plus vers une époque de la fiction où les problèmes de l'écriture seront envisagés lucidement par le romancier, et où les soucis critiques, loin de stériliser la création, pourront au contraire lui servir de moteur.[25]

We thus have yet again a self-conscious art form, given over as hostage to its own methods, and dominated by its own theory.

IV

'Would you like to go abroad?
Pollock: 'No, I don't see why the problems of modern painting can't be solved here as well as elsewhere.'

I would like to conclude by looking in rather more detail at a specific example of the move away from modernism, by the deliberate avoidance of earlier styles, and the invention of a drastically simplified 'subtracting' language. The New York school of abstract expressionist painters is perhaps the earliest distinctively postmodern group to be discussed in this book, for their reputation-establishing exhibitions took place in 1946–51. They are also the symbolic if not indeed the causal agents of a great shift in the general avant-garde culture, away from its traditional home in Europe to America. They broke free of the French tradition of the well-made, domesticated easel picture, and gave painting a new content. (One can see how radical their departures were, by comparing their work with that of superficially similar contemporary European painters like Wols and de Stäel.) This was a conscious reaction, as the quotation above from Pollock suggests. American painters knew the Paris school, were very conscious of available modernist styles, and indeed worked their way through them. They destroyed the illusion of shallow depth in cubism (Picasso, Braque), rejected the complicated but clear geometry of Mondrian, transcended figurative surrealism, and produced pictures which solved the problem of progress in art by a hard-won simplification of the language of painting.

Thus the early paintings of all the abstract expressionists (both those who were to develop into 'gesture' painters and those who produced colour field paintings) show the influence of available styles. But the real search was for a new content, away from those methods of painting, like geometric abstraction and even cubism, which had become almost too easy to adopt. The surrealists (many of whom had been exiled to New York by the war) seemed to offer one way out. Miró and Dali both had retrospective exhibitions at the

Museum of Modern Art in New York in 1941–2, which showed that surrealism could take two paths, one of which (Dali's academic realism) could be firmly rejected. On the other hand the elusive 'content' of the abstract organic forms in Mirò, and also Picasso, Klee, and Arp, were particularly interesting to many New York painters.

Thus round about 1941–2, Gottlieb, Rothko, Pollock, Motherwell, and Baziotes were all experimenting with surrealist automatism. But they had moved beyond its rather restrictive Freudianizing ideology, and were more interested in its relationship to myth and to primitive art, and to the revelation of the unconscious through universal symbols (as Jung had suggested was possible).[26] Thus Gottlieb, Rothko, and Newman asserted that they were 'concerned with primitive myths and symbols that continue to have meaning today. Only that subject matter is valued which is tragic and timeless. That is why we profess kinship with primitive and archaic art.'[27] Pollock also said that he was 'particularly impressed' by the European Moderns' 'concept of the source of art being the unconscious'.[28] The pictures produced in this light were not highly innovatory in formal terms, but they do signify a reliance upon the subjective response, particularly that which was supposed to lie below consciousness, which was crucially important for later developments. These rather complicated general assumptions will perhaps make more sense if we follow them through with reference to a single painter, Jackson Pollock, who worked through this symbolic phase to an abstract art of pure gestural expression. The work of two other New York painters, Newman and Rothko, who took another direction, into colour field painting, will be discussed further on.

The influences upon Pollock's early paintings are fairly clear; from Picasso and Mirò and Masson in particular. For example, the Mirò-like head in *Shorthand Figure* (1942), the *Guernica*-like animal of *Horse* (1945), or the Picasso-like drawing of *Pasiphäe* (1943), which is probably also influenced by Masson. Cubism sometimes suggests an underlying geometric planar design, as in *Guardians of the Secret* (1943) or *Moon Woman* (*c.* 1943).[29] These formal influences upon design and drawing are further complicated by Pollock's interest in primitive myth and symbolism seen from a Jungian point of view. (He was in Jungian analysis in 1939.)[30] Thus the totemic rearing vertical shapes of some of these paintings may have been thought of as phallic, under the influence of Indian sexual imagery. Indeed the design, patterns, and emblems of *The She-Wolf* (1943) and *Guardians of the Secret* may well stem from Indian sand painting as it influenced the Spanish colonial art of New Mexico. [See Pl. 1.]

Now the differences between the representational imagery of these paintings and the later 'drip' paintings, in which Pollock drew with paint spilt over the canvas, are obviously radical. But there are some transitional works in which the earlier style, with its too visible influences, is almost literally hidden behind the new one. Thus Pollock's movement towards the 'overall' image and its purer implications is seen in *Gothic* (1944) and *Sounds in the Grass: shimmering substance* (1946), particularly in the latter, in which 'mythic' images are overlaid by a mass of white brush strokes, so that enigmatic fragments of linear totem images seem to appear through them.

By *Cathedral* (1947) and *Full Fathom Five* (1947), whose 'sea change' works magnificently upon the drawing pins, pennies, cigarettes, paint tube tops, and matches which can just be seen embedded in its surface, Pollock had arrived at the thrown or dribbled technique of painting, by which, as De Kooning generously conceded, he 'broke the ice' of avant-garde advance. This radically new texture for abstract painting proved remarkably difficult to assimilate, as the remarks of a distinguished panel of commentators published in *Life* magazine show. *Cathedral* was described as suitable 'for an enchanting printed silk', as 'like a panel for a wall paper' and as 'a pleasant design for a necktie'. One panellist even produced the most typical of insults to avant-garde work—'I suspect any picture I could have made myself.'[31] And yet it is hardly surprising that such desperate attempts were made to assimilate Pollock's painting to the already known, for the new technique and complete abstraction went together: it allowed for a renunciation of figurative content and its problems, and indeed of past tradition (though late Monet is often very plausibly cited as at least analogous to Pollock). Nevertheless the process did not entirely involve any memory-obliterating surrender, either to a fixed and rigid method, or to pure automatism. For as Pollock himself remarked 'It seems to be possible to control the flow of the paint to a great extent . . . I don't use the accident—'cause I deny the accident.'[32] [See Pl. 2.]

It should be noted that the evolution of painting in New York in this earlier period thus took place, not by looking back to earlier painting, but as the result of artistic decisions (and abdications from them) within the picture space. Hence Harold Rosenberg's famous observation that 'at a certain moment the canvas began to appear to one American painter after another as an arena in which to act—rather than as a space in which to reproduce, design, analyse, or "express" an object, actual or imagined. What was to go on the canvas was not a picture but an event.'[33]

The idea was that a painting produced by gesticulation upon or over a canvas would be inherently expressive of the personality of the artist, who 'discovered' a picture in the very process of its making. Thus Pollock's arabesque, free-wheeling lines, which combine to create a frontal field of paint webs, are immensely expressive of mood, from the shattered, anxious, and jagged, to the more nearly graceful, decorative, and fragile. Indeed there is a dialectic in his painting, between the anarchic and 'messy' (which has been extremely influential) and the decorative and elegant. For reasons which have to do with the later evolution of painting, the latter has been rather frowned upon. But this is to ignore, it seems to me, the purely pleasurable aspect of Pollock's work, which makes him, as a colourist, a great successor to the impressionists. In any case the violence originally attributed to these pictures (partly out of shock at their method of composition, and partly because of journalistic attention to Pollock's rather drunken and violent life-style) isn't always 'there', though a feeling of movement and energy certainly is, largely because the eye has nowhere to settle, even when as often happens, broad patches of darker colour link solidly beneath the webs of dripped paint. (The most majestic example of this is the processional *Blue Poles* of 1953, which was seen as regressive when first exhibited precisely because it had a linear organization.)

These works are remarkable in their historical context for what they have subtracted from earlier painting, including Pollock's own. They do not define representative images, or outline planes, their surface is not sectioned off into separately characterized areas, there are no climactic areas of colour intensity, no field and ground relationships, no focal points to settle upon. The complexity and apparent indeterminacy of the surface texture is overwhelming, yet the eye is moved, if not to seek for order, at least to try to penetrate to the depths (or apparent depths) of the canvas, or to fasten upon some Rorschach-like relationships within the over-all field which (partly because of the huge scale of the work) it knows have nothing to do with the formal organization of the whole.

This was recognized by Pollock; 'Abstract painting is abstract. It confronts you. There was a reviewer a while back who wrote that my pictures didn't have any beginning middle or end. He didn't mean it as a compliment, but it was. It was a fine compliment.'[34] Pictures like this not only lack 'beginning middle and end' (like the music and literature we have already looked at) but their very frame fails to limit the picture space, because the huge scale of the work engulfs the spectator and thus forces part of the painting into his peripheral vision. (This was an effect which was most explicitly and effectively exploited later by Morris Louis.) Thus, as Robert Motherwell noted, 'the large format, at a blow, destroyed the century-long tendency of the French to domesticate modern painting, to make it intimate.'[35] Pollock, as he himself emphasized in a Guggenheim Fellowship application of 1947 (refused) had moved 'from easel to mural'.

From representational painting right into analytical cubism, and geometrical abstraction, there had seemed to be an answer to the question 'What is this part doing here?' Abstract painting like Pollock's cannot be interrogated in the same way, even if it can offer satisfactions as profound as any other. Many of the older conventions for 'harmony' and relation were thus overthrown. Pollock's is an art, like that of Stockhausen and Robbe-Grillet, which disorientates, and leaves far more for the spectator to do.

As I have tried to show, gestural expressionism is the result of a continued experimental evolution away from available modernist styles to the point at which the question asked above makes no sense at all. So radical was this change, that the abstract expressionist movement as a whole was attacked for 'having resigned from all the complexities of mind which Europe still regards as the *sine qua non* of artistic seriousness' and having thus 'brought modern painting to an end'.[36] This is both complaint and prophecy, and we shall encounter it again in the postmodern period. But its prediction at least is false; for much later painting defines itself in relation to the abstract expressionist movement of Pollock, Rothko, Kline, Motherwell, and Baziotes, which not only took its place in art history, but also gave rise to a critical terminology which, although vital in a period in which abstract expressionists were neglected or attacked, itself came to influence later developments, sometimes to an absurd degree. Terms like 'all-overness' and 'flatness' took upon themselves all the force of a chauvinistic academic orthodoxy, as they were used by the critical establishment to help define a distinctively American school of painting.[37] Thus even if Johns's targets later went back to representation and a new (and banal) subject-matter, they were at least still 'flat'.

Indeed with many of the paintings of the New York school we are brought up against a paradox, which seems to condition the production of much postmodern painting, and which we shall have to examine in later chapters. This is, that the more abstract and autonomous the art, the more the critic's verbalizations are made to intervene between the work and the viewer, to the point (in conceptual art, but also in the abstract geometry of Stella) at which the value of the work may be fatally confused with the critical response which it seems to specify.

PART TWO: EXPOSITION

Comme le public ne connaît du charme, de la grâce, des formes de la nature que ce qu'il en a puisé dans les poncifs d'un art lentement assimilé, et qu'un artiste original commence par rejeter ces poncifs, M et Mme Cottard, image en cela du public, ne trouvaient ni dans la sonate de Vinteuil, ni dans les portraits du peintre, ce qui faisait pour eux l'harmonie de la musique et la beauté de la peinture. Il leur semblait que le pianiste jouait la sonate qu'il accrochait au hasard sur le piano des notes que ne reliaient pas en effet les formes auxquelles ils étaient habitués, et que le peintre jetait au hasard des couleurs sur ses toiles.

Inasmuch as the public cannot recognise the charm, the beauty, even in the outlines of nature, save in the stereotyped impressions of an art which they have gradually assimilated, while an original artist starts by rejecting those impressions, so M and Mme Cottard, typical, in this respect, of the public, were incapable of finding either in Vinteuil's sonata or in Biche's portraits, what constituted harmony for them in music or beauty in painting. It appeared to them, when the pianist played his sonata, as though he were striking haphazard from the piano a medley of notes which bore no relation to the musical forms to which they themselves were accustomed, and that the painter simply flung his colours haphazard upon his canvas.
    Proust: *Du Côte de chez Swann*, trans. C.K. Scott-Moncrieff.

Chapter Two: I. The Serialist Idea

Nothing is likely about masterpieces, least of all whether there will be any. Nevertheless, a masterpiece is more likely to happen to the composer with the most highly developed language. This language is serial at present . . .
Igor Stravinsky, *Conversations*.[1]

As Susan Sontag pointed out long ago, 'a new mode of didacticism has conquered the arts, is indeed the "modern" element in art'.[2] Avant-garde art has traditionally given thrust to its own evolution by manifesto and exhortation; but the new mode Miss Sontag points to is a much severer affair. The basic style is that of the 'interventionism' we looked at earlier; if technique will not simply evolve, then it will have to be invented *ab extra*, and the human sensibility will have to march along with it as best it can. For as didacticism becomes the dominant mode, obsessed more and more with technique and less and less with traditional types of 'human expressivity', there may be a price to pay, in the loss of the idea of the work of art as giving a familiar pleasure.

It seems appropriate to begin discussion of this theme with music, an art which above all others has to be concerned with its own technical procedures, since its medium is not shared, as are the image and natural language, with non-aesthetic modes of communication. As we have already noted, the work of the twelve-note school was accepted by many composers in the 1950s as wholly revolutionary, if not in its practice, then in its implications, as attempting to specify a new language for music and workable rules for its use. Thus Pierre Boulez, one of those who proved to be most committed to the Viennese principle of logical development, asserted that with atonality 'music moved out of the world of Newton and into the world of Einstein. The tonal ideal was based upon a universe defined by gravity and attraction. The serial idea is based upon a universe that finds itself in perpetual expansion.'[3] Like Adorno, whom he admired, Boulez thus saw the development of musical language as a matter of historical necessity, a process as irreversible as the development of science. One may well doubt the validity of any such assumption; it nevertheless gave a particular fervour to many composers' advocacy of what was for some time a dominant aesthetic principle, that of serialism.

Serial methods are technically extremely complicated, but their underlying assumptions can I think be fairly simply explained. I have already stressed their emancipating effect, in freeing the composer from his memories of past music, and yet they also look to the past, in so far as they take off from a formalization of Schoenberg's (and particularly Webern's) achievement. The procedures of the Second Viennese School had become increasingly clear to analysts, from the beginning of the post-war period (for example in Leibowitz's *Schoenberg and his School* (1946), which was quite influential upon some composers) to 1963, when it was possible for George Perle to state a minimal set of rules for the treatment of the twelve-note row. Thus

(1) The set comprises all 12 notes of the semitonal scale, arranged in a specific linear order.
(2) No note appears more than once within the set.
(3) The set is stateable in any of its linear aspects: prime, inversion, retrograde and retrograde inversion.
(4) The set, in each of its four transformations (i.e. linear aspects) is stateable on any degree of the semitonal scale.[4]

It should be noted that such rules are in fact much less restrictive than those *implicit* in earlier tonal music,[5] and that plenty of parameters remained free, so that other aesthetic criteria could be observed in order to produce a satisfying final product. But these technical refinements need not concern us; it is the basic willingness to adopt such rules for composition which is important for music produced within this tradition.

Clearly enough, they provide a description of the treatment of the 'set' in serial music, as the successor to melody or theme within tonal music. Now the melody or theme as traditionally conceived, had always carried with it harmonic implications; and had thus to some extent dictated the grammar of its own development. But the harmonic surroundings of the set are much less fully specified. Indeed the only criterion generally observed was the *avoidance* of any allusion to traditional harmony, so that the old relationships between consonance and dissonance might be totally disregarded. The crucial question for any procedure of this kind is thus a simple one, but almost impossible to answer: 'What compromises with the organization of earlier music are necessary to secure intelligibility?' After all, tonal relationships did not simply help to structure traditional music for the composer, but, most important of all, they provided it with an *implicative sequence* for the listener. Rhythmic patterning, melodic motives frequently repeated, repetition of the part as before or varied, contrasts of texture, also contributed to the same end. It seems that the Second Viennese School exploited earlier conventions for all these in the absence of tonality, so that their music remained to a large degree familiar.

Composers in the postmodern period, however, have not been willing to observe such restraints. The result was that *all* the parameters of music were subjected to a restructuring as profound as was the earlier restructuring of tonality. Our citation from Stockhausen earlier shows how radical the composer's attitude could be in this respect.

Thus not only the twelve-note or other series, but also rhythm and dynamics, were made subject to precompositional decision, their sequence decided in advance. This method runs two risks; one, of subjecting the work of art to its own theory to the extent that it may lose expressive qualities for an audience; and the other, closely related, of producing structures which are far too complex for the listener (as opposed to the analyst) to assimilate. For if the redundancy of information brought about by consonant relationships, rhythmic repetition, and so on, in earlier music facilitated perception, would not a *lack* of such redundancies tend to produce a music too complex for our response, understanding, and hence enjoyment? Would we not be, once more, 'overloaded'? Everyone agrees (Boulez included) that the hearer in all cultures perceives pitch and duration as primary pattern-forming qualities for music; but can they be manipulated in the serial method of composition to the point at which they are not really at home in any culture, except as examples of the working-out of the method, whose complexities may simply impose too great a burden on the listener's memory?

I am of course now using 'serialism' in a fairly loose sense which applies to much post-war composition, to mean music composed with a series of pitches, durations, rhythms, or forms of attack whose order in the work is to some degree predetermined. This broader view is necessary in that as a matter of historical fact, 'integral serialism' (*totally* organized music in which the order of the series may not be varied) was really only dominant in the fifties and then declined, giving way to the much less rigid methods of organization in 'free twelve note music' where notes in the series may be repeated, tonal groups may occur, and so on. But it is, as will become clear in the sequel, the general method of composition with which I am concerned here, as also with the fact that the art of music in the post-war period was one which perpetually theorized its own practice.

Such composition may be entirely divorced from 'expressive' aims, and largely controlled by ground rules. We will soon come to some examples. But the status of the rules needs to be clarified at the start. It is possible of course to invent all sorts of artificial languages,—logicians, for example, invent all sorts of rule-governed systems. But they do not confuse them with 'real life' languages, viable systems of interpersonal communication. The analogy seems not quite to hold here, of course, because music does not seem to have that semantic or referential dimension which helps us to recognize natural languages. But if one thought that the harmonic system did correspond to the needs of our perceptual systems (and indeed to our emotional responses, as the past history of music would tend to suggest) then in a sense music *would* have such a system, and its 'semantics' would be our psychological response. The question we then might ask is whether the music which renounces this earlier and familiar system, also renounces its emotional range. I will suggest much later both that it does, and that it doesn't matter, but the considerations advanced above seem worth bringing into the open, since they seem to constitute the chief barrier between the ordinary music lover and contemporary music.

Until he readjusts, he misses, to put the matter at its simplest, thematic development, implicative harmonic relationships, and repetition of material, which not only make it
possible for him to remember it (and hence anticipate its
outcomes) in a few hearings, but also provide that familiar
system of tension and relaxation which facilitates an emotional response.

These difficulties once seemed great enough for the work
of Schoenberg, Webern, and Berg; but they have been overcome—and we can hear Berg's *Three Pieces for Orchestra* or
Schoenberg's *Fourth Quartet*, let alone *Wozzeck*, as works with
a clear development and wide emotional range. However,
composers in the immediate post-war period greatly
increased such difficulties when they serialized not only the
'set' of a composition, but also its other parameters. We may
see how this was done if we look at a very short but
immensely influential work, Messiaen's *Modes de valeurs et
d'intensités* (1949). It makes very few compromises with the
perceptual needs of the listener (and to this extent it is not
typical of its composer). In it there are three twelve-note
groups or series, each consisting of all the notes of the
chromatic scale. To each group is assigned a further chromatic series of twelve durations. In addition, a series of seven
dynamic levels, and twelve types of attack, are distributed
throughout the three groups. The work differs from a purely
serial one in that whereas in a serial work the order of notes
(pitches) is fixed by the series, but its parameters are free, in
Modes, the converse holds: parameters for each note are fixed
and yet its pitch order in relation to the other notes is
relatively free. As Paul Jacobs, a brilliant performer of
contemporary piano music, notes:

Perhaps the most revolutionary aspect of the piece is that the
concepts of dynamic levels and touch are completely divorced from
conventional 'expressivity'. The three twelve note series are con-
tinually fragmented, causing the vertical combinations to change
constantly: but since each note is invariably associated with a
single dynamic level and quality of attack, the music is almost
totally static. The lowest and longest note only occurs three times
and acts as a reference point to orient the listener.[6]

The effect is close to the stereotype entertained by those hostile to contemporary music: a series of isolated combinations of notes, wholly unpredictable in their relationships of pitch duration and dynamic. The most one can say is that the longer ones seem to be the lower ones. Predictability of a kind could of course be achieved by following through the formal schema with a score, though this in itself would hardly constitute a musical experience, any more than reading a recipe constitutes the eating of a meal, or the critical analysis of a joke would make one laugh.

One might have expected that its lack of compromise would have made *Modes* a dead end—the demonstration of one extreme possibility for musical organization. But such was not in fact the case. Messiaen's pupil Boulez heroically set himself the task of eliminating as many as possible of the choices as still existed in this mode of composition. The result was his *Structures 1a* (1952) for two pianos, which borrowed the note order of one of Messiaen's pitch series in *Modes* and attempted to predetermine as many other aspects of the work as possible by series, in order to see how far 'l'automatisme des relations musicales' ('automatism in musical relationships') could go.[7] His methods for doing this were immensely complicated, involving figure matrices to determine not only forty-eight possible orders of the twelve notes (pitches) but also, by being read diagonally, all note durations, dynamics, and modes of attack. Any detailed analysis of the process would be extremely tedious, and in fact the work has been much discussed.[8] Boulez himself commented: 'C'était, pour moi, un essai, ce qu'on appelle le doute, le doute cartésien; remettre tout en cause, faire table rasé de son héritage et recommencer à partir de zéro pour voir comment on peut reconstituer l'écriture à partir d'un phénomène qui a annihilé l'invention individuelle.'[9] The result was a paradoxical one, which many composers since Boulez have been astoundingly willing to accept; for the music of *Structures* doesn't sound ordered at all. As Boulez himself commented, with his usual admirable lucidity concerning his own methods, we have here an 'excès d'ordre qui équivaut au désordre' ('an excess of order which is equivalent to disorder').[10] He notes a similar effect in his *Livre pour cordes*, where once again all parameters are serialized, and comments: 'Celà constitue une démarche très particulière pour moi: cette accumulation qui part d'une principe très simple et qui arrive à une situation chaotique parce qu'elle est engendrée par un matériel qui tourne sur lui-même et qui devient tellement complexe qu'il perd toute physiognomie individuelle et arrive à faire partie d'un immense chaos.'[11] Here then we have a composer who fully accepts the lack of correspondence between the wholly rationalistic methods of composition to which he subjects himself, and the ability of the hearer to make continuous perceptual sense of the chaos which results. Only intermittent aspects of the work can be reduced to order. I think Boulez might accept this, on the grounds that his work is so complex that any over-all interpretation is impossible. Indeed he often alludes to the analogy between his music and a certain type of Mallarméan and Joycean literature, and seems to see his superimposed and serialized parameters as a kind of semantic polysemy. Hence the Mallarméan title of this work (*Livre*), which is meant to be disorienting: 'pour moi, l'œuvre doit être comme un labyrinthe, on doit pouvoir s'y perdre' ('for me the work must be like a labyrinth, one must be able to lose oneself in it').[12] (The notion of the labyrinth appeals also to the new novelists, as we shall see.) Indeed this seems to be a general principle of aesthetics for Boulez: 'Que ce soit pour un livre, un tableau, ou une musique; cette polyvalence des niveaux de lecture est quelque chose qui est, pour moi, fondamentale dans mon conception de l'œuvre.'[13] The musical work is in some way then, as we shall see, like the new novel contemporary with it—it has many levels upon which it can be read, but no dominant one; a large number of independently calculated elements (series or narrative themes) that are ingeniously woven together; and one can lose oneself in it, since it need have no single harmonic 'plot', no end, and no culmination. It is composed indeed partly to see what happens to its own 'écriture'.

In the case of music, there is a risk that the work will thus seem to be a mere demonstration of the operation of rules, whose impersonality (that ideal of so many Moderns, now achieved) precludes any feeling that the composer is expressing himself. This latter consequence is in fact widely accepted. Thus Ligeti's comment upon Boulez's *Structures 1a* is very much to the point and applies equally well, it seems to me, to the *Livre*:

> Webern's interval objects . . . still contain a trace of the (discretely) 'expressive', and although the satisfaction derived from his music is the result of quite different qualities, the traces of 'expression' present at times do provide crutches for the struggling listener. All this has vanished in . . . 'Structures'; they expose to view something that in Webern already formed the nucleus: beauty in the erection of pure structures.[14]

It is sometimes difficult to see how the performance of such music can much differ from that of Tingueley's famous self-destroying machines, except that they can be repeated; for here we have marvellously calculated structures, whose operation (performance) can only result in their own chaotic internal conflict. In outer space, as we know, galaxies collide constantly in accord with immutable astronomical laws; it is the doubtful achievement of some composers to have brought the process down to earth (quite literally in the case of John Cage's *Atlas Eclipticalis* (1961–4) in which the position of notes in the score was partly determined by star charts).

The analogy I have suggested is indeed made explicit in Stockhausen's own description of one of the most extreme pre-serialized works, his *Mantra* (1970) which combines instrumental and electronic sounds. In this piece, he returns, after a gap of nearly twelve years in which his work had been more collagist and aleatoric, to what is essentially a development of the serial methods dominant in the fifties. It is a fully notated work, for two pianos, ring modulators, and antique cymbals, based on a 'mantra' containing a series of thirteen notes, a theme whose elements are never varied, but are expanded and contracted in time (duration) and space (the intervals of the series). The mantra is repeated thirteen times, each repetition announced by a cymbal sound and centring upon a different one of its notes. In order to perform his thirteen expanding operations on the mantra series, Stockhausen has developed a system of astounding complexity. For example, his expansions entailed working with thirteen different scales, only one of which is composed of the usual 88 chromatic notes of the piano, the others leaving out various of these notes (thus expanding the intervals of the original mantra). Each of the thirteen sections of the work is thus based on a different scale or mode. The mantra also has various expansions in time, from three and a half seconds to four minutes, as its note values are also mathematically varied and extended. The whole plan is absurdly complex, and seems largely to be a matter of mathematical pattern-making, which is then imposed on the (admittedly very ingenious and beautifully varied) original mantra. The sounds the pianos make are mathematically further modified by ring modulators.[15] As already noted, Stockhausen and his interviewer Jonathan Cott are led into producing extraordinary analogies for this music—it is like a bombardment with atoms; it is like an astronomical constellation: '*Mantra* as it stands is a miniature of the way a galaxy is composed.'[16] This is a curious fulfilment of Boulez's dictum quoted earlier that the 'serial idea is based upon a universe that finds itself in perpetual expansion'. It admits both to large uncertainties about the actual forms spawned by the method, and also allows liberally for a great indeterminacy of effect. It also reminds us that serious artists can create according to rules or 'laws' and at the same time implicitly abdicate from any responsibility for the consequences. However realistic this theology of artistic creation may be, it is hardly comforting.

Some general points emerge from our discussion so far. The three composers we have discussed, and others, tended to employ newly invented, and often unique sets of syntactic premises for each composition. Stockhausen in particular invents over-all forms and grammatical rules for elements which are unique to each piece he writes. Indeed estimates of the creativity of composers have depended far too much open their ability to invent such new methods of procedure.

Thus, according to some, Stockhausen gets ahead of Boulez, who is left in isolated fidelity to the more strictly serialist idea.

However this may be, it has made it very difficult for the listener to feel the presence of background conventions in much serialized music. Acquaintance with a commonly accepted style, of course, immensely facilitates functional inference, our feel for implicative relationships within music, and our ability to compare one work with another. (This applies equally well to literature and painting.) We can, it seems, achieve this for many of the works of Schoenberg, Webern, and Berg, partly, if analysts like Hans Keller are right, because tonal procedures in fact provide the 'deep structures' of many of their works.[17] But the developments in composition described above have made this security immensely more difficult to achieve. The result may be initially fairly unpleasant, in so far as blocked inference is frustrating and successful inference is satisfying. To avoid this, we are perhaps forced into a kind of passivity, which time and familiarity seem unlikely to cure. Paradoxically enough for works which are so carefully organized, our enjoyment of the part seems to be permanently cut off from any satisfying relationship to the whole. This may happen largely because, as George Rochberg notes, 'What happens at any point is the product of the preconceived organisation, but by the same token it is a chance occurrence because it is as such not anticipated by the mind that invented the mechanism and set it in motion.'[18] Even in more controlled cases, the underlying plan may not itself be perceivable, away from the score. One suspects that some of the works of the kind we have discussed are not meant so much to be understood, as to be demonstrated. The meaning of the part may indeed be tied to its function within the system that generated it, but there is no reason whatever to suppose that the listener should be aware of this system of composition in the first place. (Though there *is* a typical implicit demand that we understand the creative process here, just as there is for the very closely analogous new novel.) After all, we don't understand Beethoven by conceptualizing the scale of the piece and the rules of harmony and counterpoint; so why should we 'understand' contemporary music by looking for tone-rows, or rhythmic rows, or dynamics rows, and watching for inversions, retrogrades, and so on? The test for the aesthetic validity of the music we have discussed *has* to depend in the end upon its perceptual intelligibility, and not on any demonstration of its underlying organization.

In this section I have chiefly been concerned with the development of the serial idea, since it provided the main driving force for avant-garde music in the post-war years. But one important qualification has to be made. This is that there were many works which used serial techniques in a much less thoroughgoing manner than in the examples cited, and thus managed to compromise effectively between new discoveries for the language of music and the needs of the listener. I would cite much of the work of Luciano Berio, who was one of the first to feel that strict serialism, with its impersonality and lack of expressivity, had gone too far. Works like his *Nones* (1954), whose effects upon the listener we shall discuss later, or *Allelujah II* (1956–8) lack nothing in drive and emotional expressivity, though this is of an unconventional kind. Messiaen, too, continued to develop as a composer in a manner far removed from that of *Modes*. Indeed he makes it clear that serial procedures are a carefully integrated rather than dominant element in his work:

Certaines de mes dernières œuvres comportent également des séries mais elles n'ont pas du tout la sonorité que l'on s'attend à trouver dans un déroulement sériel, et elles n'ont pas davantage 'l'esprit sériel'; elles restent colorées car, poussé par mon amour de la couleur, je les traite comme des couleurs.[19]

This concern for coloration gives all his works an immensely dramatic effect, which stems largely from his superb ear for contrasts of orchestration and from his rhythmic invention. The *Turangalila-Symphonie* (1949), for example, in which a large orchestra is complemented by piano and Ondes Martenot, is a true extension of both the myth and the music of Tristan and Isolde. It is in many ways related to the nineteenth-century symphony and symphonic poem. As its

(Sanskrit) title indicates it is a song of love and a hymn to joy. It has four sharply characterized and thus easily recognizable main cyclic themes which run through the work in various transformations. Its serial elements are chiefly to do with its rhythmic organization, for example in 'Chant D'Amour I' which is based on Indian tala rhythms in progressive augmentation, and in 'Turangalila II' and 'Turangalila III' in which Messiaen uses chromatic series of rhythms (in which the values increase step by step).[20] His virtuosity in thus combining serial rhythmic complexity and strong forward movement is remarkable. As in *The Rite of Spring* (which Messiaen and his pupils much studied for its rhythms) there are metrical complexities which begin by challenging the listener and end by satisfying him. In works like this (admittedly not very advanced) and his later ones, which are, there is no hint of that over-organized chaos which we found earlier. This is of course largely due to the fact that Messiaen does not usually attempt the simultaneous serialization of more than one musical parameter. This is important, as there is good reason to doubt whether such simultaneous serialization of dynamics, pitch, and duration, can ever be clearly perceived. They are not, as some composers would have us believe, 'really equivalent' to one another, and therefore organizable into separate scales which remain perceptible when used in combination.[21]

Messiaen's next purely orchestral work, *Chronochromie* (1960), represents a further advance, from the traditional symphonic forms (for example sonata form and the scherzo, still discernible in the *Turangalila-Symphonie*) to a form based on the structure of the Greek choral lyric, of strophe, antistrophe, and epode. This work is also very largely based on rhythmic series, three superimposed permutations of 32 chromatic durations,[22] which make for a great rhythmic complexity. Within this controlling serialized structure, the main elements of the work are concerned with contrasts of instrumental timbre, that 'colouring of time' to which the title of the work and Messiaen's remarks cited earlier refer. Bird songs also contribute a very fluid, clearly contoured, and repetitive thematic element. This is at its most complex in the extraordinary epode section, just before the final coda, which is not in fact subjected to serial rhythmic procedures. Here eighteen solo strings all play different bird songs. The texture is thus of an awesome complexity. It seems almost as chaotic as some of the music discussed earlier, and yet, since the section is thematically motivated and indeed impressionistic, the listener can on different hearings discern different strands of bird song. Messiaen defends this section of the work, which caused such scandal in early performances, by comparing it to the dawn chorus: 'Celà existe dans la nature, surtout au lever du jour' ('This exists in nature, above all at daybreak').[23] This is of course hardly Ravel's version of the matter; and yet Messiaen's impressionistic naturalism is typical of his music, even if it may be pointed out that the timbre of strings is hardly like that of birds.

Thus, despite the many difficulties we have encountered in pure serialist theory, our conclusions concerning its influence in the longer run, can be fairly optimistic. We may indeed feel as Stravinsky did in the passage cited from him at the outset, that serialist techniques have provided composers with a highly developed musical language, provided only that expressivity is allowed to outweigh theory. Thus in the swing away from integral serialism, 'Rigid principles gave way to free invention, structuralism was abandoned for fantasy, complexity yielded to simplification . . . [and] a new, free music evolved . . . more varied and spontaneous, and with deeper emotive foundations.'[24] Reginald Smith Brindle, whom I follow here, and who is himself an authority on serial method, points to works like Berio's *Serenata I*, Boulez's first *Improvisation sur Mallarmé*, and others by Nilson, Pousseur, and Bussotti, as examples of this 'free twelve note music' which has perhaps become the norm for the notated music of the postmodern period. It remains the point of departure, not only for the works just cited, but also for a number of those we shall encounter in later chapters.

Chapter Two: II. The New Novel

Dans la forêt enchantée du langage, les poètes vont tout exprès pour se perdre, et s'y enivrer d'égarement, cherchant les carrefours de signification, les échos imprévus, les rencontres étranges; ils ne craignent ni les détours, ni les surprises, ni les ténèbres;—mais le veneur qui s'y excite à courre la vérité, à suivre une voie unique et continue, dont chaque élément soit le seul qu'il doive prendre pour ne perdre le piste, ni le chemin parcouru, s'expose à ne pas capturer enfin que son ombre. Gigantesque, parfois, mais ombre tout de même.
Paul Valéry, *Discours* (1937).[25]

The novel, with its tendency to elaborate humanly populated and emotionally significant worlds, has been very resistant to the dominance of theory over art. Indeed Beckett and Robbe-Grillet, two of the most original and dominating writers of this period, dramatize this antithesis, between experimental evolution based on the grimmest kind of realism (as Beckett's work produces barer and yet barer analyses of the human condition) and theory in battle with traditional content (as the novels of Robbe-Grillet attempt to square up to their own critical manifestos). No small part of the achievement of these two writers has been to bring prose writing back into the avant-garde.

This new experimentalism derives very largely from the most self-regarding elements in the modernist tradition. As Henry James remarked some time ago, 'it is arrived in truth, the novel, late at self-consciousness; but it has done its utmost ever since to make up for lost opportunities'.[26] His successors have often been very acutely conscious of their own procedures, and of the need of the reader to be aware of them as well. Joyce is the most obvious example of a writer who challenges us to discover his own hidden design. Just as important for later developments was that line of works more overtly concerned with their own process of creation, which runs from Gide's *Les Faux-Monnayeurs* with its associated *Journal* to Natalie Sarraute's *Les Fruits d'or*. In other novels in which the hero is aesthete as much as writer, he too may be thought of as acquiring the experience and the modes of controlling it that will enable him to write; hence the essentially recursive forms of *À la recherche du temps perdu*, the

Portrait of the Artist as a Young Man, and *La Nausée*. These novels, though more indirect than Gide's, contribute like his to a kind of instability in the very text of the novel, and involve the reader in new ways with the very process of creation. The ghost of Tristram Shandy presides over all, and it is in fact this particular mode of fiction about fiction which has had many postmodern exemplars.

For many contemporary writers, Jorge Luis Borges is the great predecessor. Joyce, as we shall see, contributes a sense of linguistic texture; but Borges, acknowledged or not, was the first to adopt certain types of narrative handling with which we are now all too familiar. For example, in his fantasy on 'Tlön, Uqbar, orbis tertius'. This story is concerned with the competition between fictional systems and structures. In it, we find that the literature of an imaginary world (Uqbar) which itself only seems to exist in a series of encyclopaedia entries evolved by a secret society of scholars, turns out to refer to entirely imaginary regions (Mlejna and Tlön). The complication of this sentence but weakly mirrors Borges's tale, itself 'born of the conjunction of a mirror with an encyclopaedia'.

The 'facts' to which Borges purports to refer here and elsewhere are frequently so outlandish, so erudite, that we have no means of making a clear distinction between fact and fiction, or between dream, game, and waking fantasy. As in the fable of Tlön, an imagined literature may come to usurp the known universe. The proliferation of imaginary and historical narrative here, and elsewhere of perceptions of the external world (as in 'Funes the Memorious') threatens to become an overwhelming and claustrophic nightmare, of a kind we find later exploited with fiendish elaboration in the work of Thomas Pynchon.

In 'The Garden of Forking Paths' we read of a man, Ts'ui Pen, who set out to make a book and a labyrinth—and only the narrator discovers his secret, that the book itself *is* the labyrinth, within whose plot time itself 'forks' so that various possible futures are envisaged. (Robbe-Grillet in his later novel, *Dans le Labyrinthe*, warns us of this at the outset.) This story, first published in 1941 in book form, merits close attention, for it is prophetic of one of the directions which fiction was later to take.

Its enclosing 'plot' is very simple. A Chinese-born German spy living in England is being hunted down by an English officer. Before being caught he must reveal to his German chief the location of a British artillery park. He achieves this by murdering an elderly sinologist, Stephen Albert, so that when his crime is reported in the newspapers, his chief may infer that his target lies in the town of Albert. (This whole story is 'authenticated' at the outset by learned references to Liddell Hart's history of the First World War.) But the centre of Borges's story lies in the discussion between the narrator Yu Tsun and Albert, concerning the novel called 'The Garden of Forking Paths' written long ago by Ts'ui Pen, who withdrew from society for thirteen years to construct a labyrinth. It is the sinologist Albert who has discovered that this labyrinth is in fact a novel; and it has features which have since become very familiar to us in the work of Robbe-Grillet and others:

> In all fictional works, each time a man is confronted with several alternatives, he chooses one and eliminates the others; in the fiction of Ts'ui Pen, he chooses—simultaneously—all of them. He *creates*, in this way, diverse futures, diverse times which themselves also proliferate and fork. Here, then, is the explanation of the novel's contradictions. Fang, let us say, has a secret; a stranger calls at his door; Fang resolves to kill him. Naturally, there are several possible outcomes; Fang can kill the intruder, the intruder can kill Fang, they both can escape, they both can die, and so forth. In the work of Ts'ui Pen, all possible outcomes occur; each one is the point of departure for other forkings. Sometimes, the paths of this labyrinth converge: for example, you arrive at this house, but in one of the pasts you are my enemy, in another, my friend.[27]

One might note that, typically for Borges, the narrative mode has a fantastic metaphysico-philosophical rationalization (whereas the techniques of the later *nouveau roman* are on the whole not thus explained, and simply remain autonomous features of the work of art). Thus Ts'ui Pen believes that different times run parallel, occasionally diverging or converging. All possibilities really exist in the one universe. Thus in the present time of Borges's story 'which a favourable fate has granted me, you have arrived at my house; in another, while crossing the garden, you found me dead; in still another, I utter these same words, but I am a mistake, a ghost'.[28]

The work of many new novelists in France is in many ways a huge extension of Borges's method here (though often without his economy of structure, or his wit and humour). They too believe in the causal arbitrariness of narrative method such as it is outlined in the story we have just looked at. But this is only one aspect (though perhaps the most obvious one) of their methods. The other, equally crucial, is the notion of the novel as a linguistic construct.

The dominance of theory here (and its associated critical practices) is quite remarkable. The central notion is that of a text whose own methods of composition are designed to test and indeed break previously accepted codes of communication, rather than to assert any stable relationship of the text to the external (or fictional) world. Thus the new novel may be a dramatization of the phenomenology of the creative process. This is assumed to be of central interest, in an age in which the novel is no longer needed (it is thought) to provide mundane information about the world, its characters, and environment. This function may be given over entirely to psychology, sociology, newspapers, television, and so on. A more severe and recently more dominant version of this argument asserts that it is not simply the creative process which is at issue (this is far too psychological) but the possibilities of the language itself, which the creative process exploits. Hence my epigraph from Valéry, which could be supported by others from poets like Auden, to show that this idea is not in essence new. What is new is the demand for that kind of attention to prose (in terms of repeated words, themes, syntactic features, etc.) which had previously chiefly been accorded to poetry.[29] The work of art thus conceived does not point beyond itself to some external reality; it is a text which exposes to us the forms by which we make the real intelligible, and shows up these means for the artificial con-

ventions they are. This type of writing is thus in alliance with
that acute suspicion of the mimetic or referential function of
language which we find in the work of Roland Barthes,
particularly when he reveals in *S/Z* that even realist conventions, for example in Balzac's story 'Sarrasine', which he
subjects to an extended and virtuosic analysis, are really just
as fictional as any others. 'Le réalisme . . . ne peut donc être
la copie des choses, mais la connaissance du langage;
l'œuvre la plus "réaliste" ne sera celle qui "peint" la réalité,
mais qui . . . explorera le plus profondément possible la
réalité irréelle du langage.'[30]

The novel is thus held to dramatize the possibilities of its
own form and medium. This is seen as a revolutionary
development, as irreversible as that discerned by Boulez in
music, by critic–writers like Philippe Sollers: 'ce qui a été
appelé "littérature" appartient à une époque close laissant
place à une science naissante, celle de l'écriture.'[31] There is a
remarkable agreement on this among creative writers, for
example Claude Simon, who says that 'il me semble que le
livre se fait au niveau de l'écriture' ('it seems to me that a
book is made at the level of writing')[32] and that the process of
composition is that of 'mot après mot par l'acheminement
même de l'écriture' ('word after word along this same path of
writing').[33] All this, as I have said, jibes very well with the
typical assumption of structuralist critics that 'Le texte par-
ticulier ne sert qu'une instance qui permet de décrire les
propriétés de la littérature.'[34]

Much inspiration for these points of view was derived
from one of our transitional works, *Finnegans Wake* ('usylessly
unreadable') whose very 'illisibilité' and resistance to univocal interpretation showed that it dramatized the language
itself.[35] Precisely because we can't see through the *Wake* to
the construction of a single mimetically consistent world, we
are perpetually made aware of it as a second order, self-
conscious manipulation of language. What we learn in reading it is as much about some of the bizarre potentialities of
syntax, semantics, and historical etymology as anything
else. Like the novels of Robbe-Grillet or Simon, it offers no
consistently dominating *points de repère* from which we can

disambiguate its metaphors. As Jacques Derrida pointed out, Joyce's 'écriture'

ne traduit plus une langue dans l'autre à partir de sens communs, mais circule à travers toutes les langues à la fois, accumule leurs energies, actualise leurs consonances le plus secrètes, décèle leurs plus lointains horizons communs, cultive les synthèses associatives au lieu de les fuir et retrouve la valeur poétique de la passivité.[36]

In Joyce, system is piled upon system, and all are seen as equivalent, just as no single point of view in *La Maison de rendezvous* or *Triptyque* is allowed to be dominant—and in both types of work, as we shall see, the linkage between part and part is in fact linguistic.

But of course the 'new novel' (as it was called long ago) is not a single genre, as conventionalized as the Petrarchan sonnet. Its major practitioners (to my mind Michel Butor, Robbe-Grillet, and Claude Simon) are wholly individual in their methods and outlook. There seem also to be two types of novel involved here, corresponding in some degree to the phases of its historical development, the first phenomenological in the tradition of *La Nausée*, the text still 'recuperable' as a psychological study, and a second type, in which the notion of any dominating consciousness (like that of Mathieu in *Le Voyeur*) is abjured, and a more complicated game with language is played, so that any naturalistic relationship between character and plot is much less easily recuperable. It seems that *La Jalousie* and *La Modification* are different from *La Maison de rendezvous* and *Triptyque* in precisely this way. It is the latter mode of writing with which I am primarily concerned here, as its experimentation is more radical.

My treatment of the new novel is thus extremely selective. It is a mode of writing which has already attracted an immense critical literature, and it would be impossible to do justice to the subtleties (and frequently enough the absurdities) of the debate concerning it. In what follows I have chosen to concentrate upon Robbe-Grillet, as the most influential and theoretically explicit of these writers, and later, upon Claude Simon, as a writer who, while extremely reticent about his own methods, seems to me to have exploited the possibilities of the new novel to the point at which it can be said to have produced the poetic master-pieces its theory demands. I am conscious that I thus omit Butor, whose early work seems to me to have combined a Balzacian–Joycean realism with a beautiful narrative ingenuity, and I much regret this.

Novels written in accord with the assumptions sketched above have notoriously caused great difficulties for their readers, and it was perhaps in the hope of mitigating them that the detective story (which also fascinated Borges) with its incorporation of the puzzled reader into the work, so often provided a model for the *nouveau roman*. Thus Butor's *L'Emploi du temps*[37] and Robbe-Grillet's *Les Gommes*, *Le Voyeur*, and *La Maison de rendezvous*, like the detective novel, involve *inter alia* the withholding of information concerning a crime from the reader, or conversely of presenting it to him repeatedly in different paradoxical contexts. The new novelists have perhaps been driven to use the detective story thread stretched out 'always so scientifically tight', to adapt Henry James's phrase, in order to hold the attention of the reader despite his bafflement. We are challenged, like the detective, to interpret evidence and to adopt hypotheses about 'what is really going on' (however much Robbe-Grillet may protest that we should not). This necessary adoption of perpetually defeated or modified hypotheses is the theoretical converse of the self-conscious narrative procedures involved in the novels. It requires, so to speak, a critical participation in the literal sense: the reader cannot simply treat the text as a mimetic window, but is forced to adopt the techniques of the critic right from the start.

Thus when John Fletcher tried to recuperate a detective story plot from *La Maison de rendezvous* he came out with this:

Johnson (also Sir Ralph and other aliases) has shady business transactions with Edouard Manneret, who is murdered under suspicious circumstances which make it imperative for Johnson to leave Hong Kong at once and return to his Macao base (he has a Portuguese passport). But he wishes to take with him one of the girls in the Maison de Rendez-vous run by Lady Ava (Eva Bergman) but this Lauren (or Loraine or Laureen, i.e. 'L' or 'elle') who is a society woman who has chosen this life as the ultimate in perversion, is determined that her price shall be exorbitant. Johnson asks Manneret (now no longer dead) to lend him the huge sum involved, and kills him when he is rebuffed, therefore he has to leave Hong Kong at once. He returns to Lady Ava's to persuade Lauren. The book ends on a Hitchcock-like twist. He rushes into her room, but finds himself face to face with the police lieutenant who has already questioned him surrounded with soldiers with guns. L looks at him—he has been betrayed.[38]

However, in order to provide this relatively consistent thread for the novel, he had to resist or eliminate a number of contradictory elements, quite apart from those of time reversal, modified and literal repetition of incidents within different contexts, and so on, which are typical of Robbe-Grillet. Thus Manneret is killed at least four times in different ways: by Johnson; by a blackmailer who discovers that Manneret sold a Japanese girl to a cannibalistic restaurant; by Kim, Lady Ava's Eurasian servant, on whom he has been testing aphrodisiacs and soporifics; and by communists whose pretext is that he is a double agent in the pay of Formosa. These are all of course clichés of the thriller,—and deliberately so, for reasons we will come to discuss later.

Robbe-Grillet, it must be said, has always resisted this kind of interpretation of his work, partly because it pays too little respect to the freedom of the artist to invent new conventions—in this he echoes Boulez and Stockhausen.[39] Indeed in his works from *La Maison de rendezvous* on, the notion of the even freer, 'ludic' novel has become central to his thinking. This deliberately exploits the narrative and thematic clichés in his work. We can see how stereotyped these can be by referring to our account above. Great emphasis is laid however on their structural interrelations, which demonstrate the free creativity of the author. This formal interest supposedly helps the reader to become free of those bourgeois, value-laden interpretations of the literary text, infected as they are by the 'dominant ideology', and which are inevitably imposed upon it if it is seen as in some way 'realistic'.

Thus the game that Robbe-Grillet plays is supposedly indifferent to content, and is designed simply to draw attention to its own procedures. 'Tout mon travail est précisément en train d'essayer de mettre en lumière ses structures' ('All my work is precisely engaged in the attempt to bring its own structures to light,'), he says.[40] The elements or counters in this game are what he calls 'thèmes genérateurs'; and he draws attention to the important parallel between his method and that of the other arts, based as they so often are in the postmodern period, upon combinatorial logic:

Ce sont en effet, désormais, les thèmes du roman eux-mêmes (objets, événements, mots, mouvements formels etc.) qui deviennent les éléments de base engendrant toute l'architecture du récit et jusqu'aux aventures qui s'y déroulent, selon un mode de développement comparable à ceux que mettent en œuvre la musique sérielle ou les arts plastiques modernes.[41]

Of course, the procedures he adopts seem not to be subordinated to any strict, and ultimately discernible underlying *plan*, as in serialist music—no critic has yet made such a scheme public, and so one may assume that they don't exist; on the other hand even serialist method often allows for a freedom at least as great as that observable in Robbe-Grillet's prose. And we do indeed have the same sense of a background of rule-governed manipulation, against which any particular incident seems purely contingent. Robbe-Grillet himself recognizes this kind of chance:

Loin de disparaître, l'anecdote se met ainsi à foisonner: discontinue, plurielle, mobile, aléatoire, designant elle-même sa propre fictivité, elle devient un 'jeu' au sens plus fort du terme.

These burgeoning anecdotal units aim at a deliberate banality, and this for interesting ideological reasons. For the 'thèmes générateurs', simple objects or incidents though they may be, are frequently enough selected for their cliché-ridden 'mythological' status, and this gives their manipulator a clear mimetic commitment:

Je les prends volontiers, quant à moi, parmi le matériau mythologique qui m'environne dans mon existence quotidienne.

They may be 'faits divers . . . vitrines . . . affiches' for
lorsque j'accomplis un parcours dans les couloirs du métropolitan,
je me trouve assailli par une multitude de signes dont l'ensemble
constitue la mythologie du monde ou je vis, quelque chose comme
l'inconscient collective de la société, c'est à dire à la fois l'image
qu'elle veut se donner d'elle-même et le reflet des troubles qui la
hantent.

This is a kind of Jung updated, modified by a Pop-art
acceptance of the urban environment, and a Barthesian
treatment of the thing as a sign (but without any attempt to
say what or how significant, their underlying codes may be,
for Robbe-Grillet's codes are the codes of his own writing).
The point that it does have, once we turn to the novels that
are supposed to exemplify the theory, is to suggest that the
'subconscious' of society is an irredeemably banal mixture of
sado-masochistic fantasies. As it stands, it suggests that once
all value-judgements are given up, or are seen to be infected
by bourgeois assumptions (*a priori* bad) then we must sink
through the culture to the level of a 'B' movie, and a passive
acceptance of undifferentiated experience, its objects,
actions, and events, rather like an anaesthetized Virginia
Woolf. It is a curious response to the urban situation, which
has its parallels in the films of Jean-Luc Godard.

Thus typically, in *La Maison de rendezvous*, *Projet pour une
révolution à New York*, and *Glissements progressifs du plaisir* (a
film script) Robbe-Grillet takes elements that on the
dumbest level we might expect to be present in a work on a
given theme. In those cited, murder amongst drug-runners,
torture amongst revolutionaries, and satyr priests are
examples from each work respectively. These elements are
then orchestrated along with others according to his own
rules. Thus in a novel about revolutionaries, the following
incidents might occur, as John Weightman points out:[42]

—a man walks to the nearest subway station, goes to a secret
underground hall and hears a revolutionary speech
—a beautiful female half-caste is tortured to gain information
concerning a rival group
—an intruder breaks into the man's flat in his absence by climbing
up a fire escape and breaking a window.

These indeed are some of the principal events of *Projet*. They occur again and again. New York was chosen as a setting because (presumably in the unconscious fantasies of most people) it is thought that 'on y viole aussi impunemént que dans les rêves'. It thus figures in 'l'inconscient de la société' as the home of violence, just as in the earlier novel, Hong Kong is the home of drug-running and exotic brothels. Nevertheless Robbe-Grillet is quite right to insist that these clichéd facts and stereotypical actions are transformed by his free imaginative manipulations. For as in Warhol's car crashes or Marilyn faces or Coke bottles, there is an insistence on the banal image combined with a creative distortion; in the pictorial case that of the washes of light pastel colour whose connotations clash with the subject they obscure, in Robbe-Grillet's that of a causal connection which may be equally arbitrary. Robbe-Grillet's justification for his procedures would indeed apply equally well to Warhol and other 'pop' artists:

Designées en pleine lumière comme stéréotypes, ces images ne fonctionnent plus comme des pièges du moment qu'elles seront reprises par un discours vivant, qui reste le seul espace de ma liberté. Cette cité qui m'écrasait, je sais maintenant qu'elle est imaginaire; et refusant de subir en aliéné ses contraintes, ses peurs, ses phantasmes, je veux au contraire les réinvestir par ma propre imagination.

Despite this avowal, many of the stereotypes in these later three novels still manage to ensnare us for another reason; they have a clear base in sexual fantasy. One might almost say that the peculiar requirements of the genre of pornography have largely taken the place of the earlier detective story elements in retaining the interest of the reader. They are once more like Pop art, because they are treated in a very cool manner. They have the poverty of meaning of their sources, and although they occur again and again, they never quite threaten to become archetypal or symbolic in any very complex way. (They are quite different in this respect from the even more cunningly permutated imagery of Robert Coover's 'The Baby Sitter', which exploits the techniques of the new novel to devastating emotional effect.)[43] In *Projet* the breaking of a window pane and the torture of a girl are described in the same clinical and detached manner. Extreme stylistic simplicity in description goes hand in hand with a very complex ordering. This repetition with variation of key sentences may conceivably be of great linguistic interest to some (as a game is played with the Saussurian *langue* that lies behind the novelist's *parole*), but it also quickly brings about the extinction of any direct emotional response. All the elements in the following representative passage occur elsewhere:

Après avoir flairé le sang encore liquide, dont plusieurs ruisselets de longueurs inégales ont coulé sur le carrélage, et fureté de droite et de gauche aux alentours, le rat maintenant s'enhardit: il se hisse sur son train de derrière et promène en hésitant les pattes antérieures et le museau sur le corps de la suppliciée, qui gît sur le dos dans une pose amollie, abandonée, ses charmes offerts plus que dissimulées par les lambeaux lacérés rougis de la longue chemise blanche. La bête, qui semble attirée surtout par les blessures des sept poignards enfoncés dans les chairs tendres, en haut des cuisses et au bas du ventre tout autour de la toison poisseuse, la bête velue est si grosse que, tout en conservant appui sur le sol, elle parvient ainsi à explorer la fragile peau déchirée, depuis l'aine jusqu'aux environs du nombril ou la chair nue apparait à nouveau, encore intacte à cet endroit, dans un large accroc effiloché du léger tissu de lin. C'est là que le rat se décide à mordre et commence à dévorer le ventre.[44]

Once the girl victim has undergone her seven stab wounds and the rat has come or been threatened to come to lick up her blood or chew on her entrails a few times, one is either past caring or mildly sickened by the repetitive and stylized violence (distanced by the vocabulary of sub-literature—cf. 'charmes' above). It is difficult to say what formal interest these repeated passages have; very little intrinsically, and if they are there simply to exemplify the imaginative and crea-tive freedom of the writer, then this is a point that can be demonstrated at much less tedious length, as in the Coover story cited. And if all such novels are designed to demons-trate this freedom, then one is entitled to wonder what the *differentia* between them may be. The process seems to lack the interest, say, of seeing Picasso create a picture by rejecting many of its versions (as in the film by Clouzot), which is a much more prodigal and impressive demonstration of creative freedom, since we value successive states of a picture, independently, in a way that we cannot possibly value successive paragraphs of a novel. There is in fact a nihilism involved in the method that goes beyond the logician's dictum that if you contradict yourself you haven't said anything.[45]

Robbe-Grillet's attacks upon 'le sérieux' are perhaps meant to meet this sort of objection, when he asserts that the events he describes are not *supposed* to have any emotional significance or human value, for such merely human inventions must be renounced: 'Vous ne pouvez pas prétendre que je joue pour échapper au tragique puisque, au contraire, le jeu dénonce ce tragique comme étant une création humaine, qu'une autre création humaine peut détruire.'[46] The pen is clearly meant to be mightier than the sword. It is not clear whether Robbe-Grillet believes that the destruction (by his work) of such sentimental notions as that torture is a serious matter, tragic, or even wrong, may be permanent, or merely a temporary illusion produced by reading. One fears the former. It would be charitable to him to believe that he thinks such notions may be given up simply for the duration of the 'game' as it were. But even if this is so, the game is seen as destructively liberating: 'le sérieux suppose qu'il y a quelque chose derrière nos gestes: une âme, un dieu, des valeurs, l'ordre bourgeois . . . tandis que derrière ce jeu, il n'y a rien . . . le jeu s'affirme comme une pure gratuité.'[47] His method is thus tied to a further ideological concern. This can be expressed in the claim that the breaking away from emotional involvement with persons, and that sequential type of narrative which is tied to bourgeois assumptions concerning the social order is in *itself* revolutionary or liberating. This has become a commonplace amongst many French writers and critics, reflecting an alliance between the two attacks on nineteenth-century narrative led by Roland Barthes and by Robbe-Grillet. Thus according to the latter:

après la faillite de l'ordre divin (de la société bourgeoise) et, à sa
suite, de l'ordre rationaliste (du socialisme bureaucratique) il faut
pourtant comprendre que seule les organisations ludiques
demeurent possibles.
'La révolution elle-même est un jeu' comme disaient les plus
conscients des révolutionnaires de mai.[48]

This passage neatly encodes the frequent left-wing delusion
that 'after this' then 'only that' is 'possible', thus reflecting
an absurd confidence in the relationship of the theoretical
conclusions of the few to the practice of the many.

Nevertheless, 'liberation' in some less modish and more
philosophical sense has been Robbe-Grillet's aim throughout his career. Thus the notorious emphasis in the early
nouveau roman on 'chosisme' was partly a way of asserting,
contra Sartre in *La Nausée* and elsewhere, that the external
world, far from being complicit with, and defining man's
sense of his own existence, is in fact indifferent to man, who,
like the writer in Robbe-Grillet's novels, is free in the direction of his 'regard'.

Or le monde n'est signifiant ni absurde. Il *est* tout simplement . . .
autour de nous, défiant la meute de nos adjectifs animistes ou
ménagers, les choses *sont là*. Leur surface est nette et lisse, intacte,
sans éclat louche ni transparence. Toute notre littérature n'a pas
encore réussi à en entamer le plus petit coin, à en amollir la
moindre courbe.[49]

The new realism of Robbe-Grillet and others was thus as
much philosophical stance as new technique. It was also a
recasting of tradition, an attack on the straw man of
nineteenth-century narrative. Robbe-Grillet's later move
into the free play of structures, or 'écriture', can be seen as a
logical development from his earlier belief in the free play of
the mind upon things, obstinate as they are, and from his
opposition to narratives which made men seem heroic, or
tragic (as Roquentin and even Camus's Meursault may have
come to seem), or even seem to have a 'character' at all.

This aim was not of course entirely achieved in the early
novels. It is difficult to see how the psychopathological
interpretation of the characters of the narrator in *La Jalousie*

or of Mathieu in *Le Voyeur* could be simply ruled out of court. In these cases the theory and the result seem not to have been in perfect accord. Indeed Robbe-Grillet admitted that this relationship was 'dialectique' and 'assez lâche' ('pretty loose').[50] It is, as I have tried to show, in the later ludic novels that the theory of creation and of imaginative freedom begins to get a grip on the equally theory-dominated narrative procedures. The point of these is not to produce a philosophical fable about possible worlds, as we saw in the case of Borges, but to liberate the reader from bourgeois ways of seeing the world in the play of the text. It may be doubted of course whether this literature could have any very permanent effect (any more than the events of 1968 which Robbe-Grillet so much admired), and one occasionally feels that he falls into the trap that lay in wait for some of the composers we discussed earlier: of simply making the work of art the demonstration of its own methods, to the point also at which minute frustrations in our search for sequence begin to outweigh the pleasures of insight into compositional method. Robbe-Grillet is nevertheless, like Pierre Boulez, simply the most extreme, lucid, and polemical of a whole school of allies, and his achievement, along with the structuralist critics who owe so much to his example, has been to recast, albeit temporarily, the whole of the past tradition of novel-writing.

Chapter Two: III. Abstraction and Concept

the bride
Is never naked. A fictive covering
Weaves always glistening from the heart and mind.
Wallace Stevens, 'Notes Towards a Supreme Fiction'.

PAINTING n. The art of protecting flat surfaces from the weather
and exposing them to the critic.
Ambrose Bierce, *The Devil's Dictionary*.

In literature, there is a natural alliance between text and
critical theory. Since they employ the same linguistic mode
of discourse, the one can easily incorporate or imply the
other. But the connection between the plastic arts and language seems more paradoxical. How do we cross over from a
non-linguistic mode to a linguistic one? In fact, as I suggested in my opening chapter, postmodern painting soon
developed a very close relationship to critical discourse,
which has been used to guide, promote, and justify a bewil-
deringly fast turnover of styles. The visitor to the art gallery
has been encouraged to orient himself by interposing a conceptual schema, often a very misty or even foggy one, between himself and the work of art. He has had to adjust to a
new critical vocabulary as much as to a new visual style, and
indeed the work's own power to survive within the politics of
the avant-garde, its ability to establish lines of influence, has
too often depended upon its critical implications, rather than
its intrinsic interest as an 'aesthetic object'.

This relationship is at its most strained in the case of
abstract art. The mimetic work deals with a world which has
already been appropriated to linguistic or indeed literary
description and can thus imply them. But abstract objects in
themselves do not figure in our world in the way in which
people, landscapes, or even food and objects of domestic use
do. They can be described, of course, and as we shall see,
they can be generated by linguistically expressed rules; but
they do not naturally figure within the drama of life. (I do not
deny of course that as objects for contemplation they can add
immensely to its pleasures.) That is why, for example, Mondrian's claims to revolutionize society through abstract art

seem so extraordinary. History has now diminished his work to its bars and rectangles; they are immensely beguiling as decorative designs and as objects for contemplation of a private kind; but they are not *used* by mankind in such a way as to revolutionize society, in anything like the way that the proponents of De Stijl might have hoped.[51]

Nevertheless, this grand tradition in which abstract work is made ideologically significant, seems to have been of great importance for the abstract expressionists, and particularly for Barnett Newman. One might be led to suppose, that from the decorative point of view, many of Newman's paintings are 'nothing but' a strip running vertically down a plain colour field. The technique here may derive partly from Mondrian's use of tapes; but we have here, once more, a drastic simplification. For the complex harmonies of Mondrian have given way to the definition of single intervals, as in the huge 8′ by 8′ square at the centre of *Vir heroicus sublimis* (1950–1). (This is not the only mark of the independence of such painting from the past; its over-all size, 8′ by 18′, makes it a museum piece rather than a domestic picture for the art market, of which Newman had at that time despaired.) Such painting had a great formal influence; but this is not the way in which Newman himself saw the matter (though one has to allow in all quotations from him for his sophisticated sense of humour):

. . . if I have made a contribution, it is primarily in my drawing. I hope that I have contributed a new way of seeing through drawing . . . Instead of working with the remnants of space, I work with the whole space. Almost fifteen years ago Harold Rosenberg challenged me to explain what one of my paintings could possibly mean to the world. My answer was that if he and others could read it properly it would mean the end of all state capitalism and totalitarianism. That answer still goes.[52]

The oddly dogmatic and assertive tone of this should not deceive us into thinking that Newman had not thought long and deeply about his art. Indeed his extended monologue essays show that his work proceeded in the light of profound philosophical meditation. Newman deliberately set himself to analyse the past history of painting; thus for example he attacks Mondrian's work at some length in his 'The Plasmic Image' of 1942–5, as 'founded upon bad philosophy and bad logic' and for trying to 'reduce the world to its basic shape' of horizontal and vertical lines.[53] Newman calls his new, adversary painting 'plasmic'

because the plasmic elements of the art have been converted into mental plasma. The effect of these new pictures is that the shapes and colours act as symbols to [elicit] sympathetic participation on the part of the beholder with the artist's thought . . . The new painter owes the abstract artist a debt for giving him his language, but the new painting is concerned with a new kind of abstract thought.[54]

Newman thus goes beyond the concept of abstract painting as even remotely derived from 'nature' as in Mondrian or Kandinsky, and paints the 'idea'; for example in his series of *Stations of the Cross* exhibited in the Guggenheim Museum in 1966. Yet his paintings are often in a relationship to their titles, or names, or 'ideas', that even Wittgenstein (for one) would find puzzling. For example, how does *Adam* differ from *Abraham*, or indeed *Tundra*? (Or do we have to say that this is the wrong question to ask, that the title doesn't implicitly describe or connote anything anyway, but simply points to or identifies an individual object? The titles would then just be proper names in something like the familiar logician's sense, identifying the members of a family of objects with a common feature of design.) Newman himself said that his aim was to make the title, often bestowed long after the painting was finished, reflect his 'idea' in a different sense, as 'a metaphor that described my feelings when I did the painting'.[55] But this is just as problematic. What for example is the 'feeling' of *Tundra* as opposed to that of *Abraham* or of *Onement I*? [See Pl. 3.]

These perplexities and doubts have not much appealed to critics, who have tended to claim diverse symbolic properties for Newman's paintings taken in conjunction with their titles, regardless of their similarities in form and content. Thus Hess, in discussing *Onement I* (1948), the painting in which Newman settled upon his format of the rectangle divided by a vertical stripe, sees it as 'a complex symbol, in the purest sense, of Genesis itself'. It is, he says, 'an *act* of division, a *gesture* of separation, as God separated light from darkness, with a line drawn in the void.'[56] The red-orange stripe is, further, a Cabbalistic metaphor for the fashioning of the first man, the only animal that walks upright, out of the earth, which is represented by the darker red ground that the stripe bisects ('Adamah' in Hebrew means earth).

This type of criticism sees the painting as an act of creation, which, apart from re-emphasizing that self-reflective quality of art in postmodernism that we have already had occasion to refer to, is also peculiarly consonant with the approach to abstract expressionist painting in this period that we cited earlier from Rosenberg; in seeing it as inherently gestural and as creating out of nothing because it is (mimetically) indebted to nothing.

One might retort on the other hand that it is much easier to see what these paintings are *not*: and that it is extremely difficult to add to their negative specification the symbolic resonances claimed by Hess, who himself has to admit that 'Newman never spoke about such a basis for his art'.[57] They are really much meditated simplifications of all earlier abstract art. In fact Newman himself defines them in a negative way, that of subtraction from a given language, which we have emphasized earlier in discussing the independence of post-war art from modernism. He says that they are 'Not space cutting nor space building [of cubism] not construction nor fauvist destruction; not the pure line, straight and narrow [of Mondrian and other geometricists] not the tortured line, distorted and humiliating [of expressionism]; not the accurate eye, all fingers [of realism] not the wild eye of dreams, winking [of academic surrealism].'[58] One might add that in contrast to his contemporaries too, Newman forgoes the atmospheric illusionism of Rothko and Baziotes, and the rich texture found in many abstract expressionists, in favour of an austere, puritanical art, distanced as far as possible from any specific imagery. His example has been influential—particularly upon later colour-field painters like Kelly, Louis, Noland, and Stella, who also produced an art without obvious visual appeal, in deliberate simplification of the chaos and multiplicity of modernism.[59] Painting like that of Newman showed them a way of escape from the expressionist *Angst*-ridden style; their art is thus at the opposite pole from that of Pollock and De Kooning. They sought an art which was emotionally disengaged, formally rigorous, and existentially anonymous. As Lawrence Alloway pointed out, 'Jasper Johns' targets of 1955, Noland's circles from late 1958, and Stella's symmetrical black paintings from 1958–9 on are . . . significant shifts from the directional brush work and projectional anxiety of the Expressionists.'[60] The result was a new variation upon the entirely non-representational abstraction; the canvas itself becomes an object, which frequently denies any relationship to the external world, even one which one might imagine to be mediated by symbolism, as in the case of Newman.

The work of Frank Stella is central to this reorientation in abstract art. Although his very early paintings (of 1958) are atmospheric in a manner reminiscent of Rothko, he quickly saw the rather simple point of Johns's targets and flags, and produced work which repudiated the complexity of organization and psychological interest of much earlier painting:

I always get into arguments with people who want to retain the old values in painting—the humanistic values they say that they always found on the canvas. If you pin them down, they always end up asserting that there is something there besides the paint on the canvas. My painting is based on the fact that only what can be seen is there. It really is an object . . .
All I want anyone to get out of my paintings, and all I ever get out of them, is the fact that you can see the whole idea without any confusion . . . what you see is what you see.[61]

This claim certainly applies well to Stella's painting in 1959, which is composed of nothing but black stripes (as in *Tomlinson Court Park*). They are often on the Newman scale, but the 'pin stripes' are symmetrically organized, and have nothing of the mystery of interval of the earlier painter. (This did not prevent William Rubin from claiming to be 'almost mesmerised by their eerie, magical presence'.)[62] They were thus 'historically important' in a way that has bothered artists and more particularly critics all through the post-modern period; after such a reduction of artistic resources, where could one go? The answer for Stella was to kink his lines and shape his canvasses. They stayed flat and regular (critically desirable attributes) but their aluminium paint-stripes now ran in parallel with canvas edges containing symmetrically placed indentations, as in *Newstead Abbey* (1960) or *Luis Miguel Dominguin* (1960). [See Pl. 4.]

This new method allowed for further series of paintings to be produced, in U, T, or H shapes (1962), and then in lavender-coloured polygons with a void at the centre, the latter exhibited in 1964, and named individually after the artist's friends, like *Carl André*. In all these paintings the 'logic' of stripe following canvas edge was preserved; and their spiritual blankness and nihilism was much remarked upon. Nevertheless, the rigour with which they followed a formula for design was undeniable. The most elementary pictorial facts are presented for our consideration, and it could be argued that there was thus also a certain mental hygiene involved, as in the earlier work of Mondrian and Newman.

The next step forward for Stella was to the relatively more complex combination of colour stripes whose forward or backward hues within a maze-like pattern imparted a mild illusionism to the canvas, as in *Jasper's Dilemma* (1962–3) which turns on the contrast between grisaille and colour. The result could be (and was) confused with Op art, though the tensions between colour values and the interlocking of the stripes in this and later work were simpler and more direct than in the complex illusionism of Op. Indeed in most of these works Stella's decision to avoid the complex rela-tional balancing of modernist painting and to stick to sym-metry, to 'make it the same all over'[63] is maintained, even if in the star-shaped canvasses of 1964, like *Plant City*, and the work based on vector shapes, like *Black Adder*, there is some tension between the velocities of the diagonals and the containing frame.

In all these works, there was a very close relationship, much emphasized by critics, between the canvas and the implied recipe for its construction. Their production as parts of series (so that one could see the current method repeated) reinforced this reaction, which discounted simplicity against critical analysis, thus allowing theory to redeem an art which otherwise ran the risk of being accused of extreme banality.

In 1967–8 a profound change took place in Stella's art. He worked to a new modulus, that of the circle and its parts, and moved way beyond any claims to symmetry or immediate apprehension. *Tahkt – I – Sulayman I* (1967), for example, is designed like a polyptych, and contains a balance of forms which is indeed complex and relational so far as the geometry and the colour segmentation goes. As Rosenblum remarks, 'the eye and the mind are at first simply dumbfounded by the sheer multiplicity of springing rhythms, fluorescent Day-Glo colour and endlessly shifting planes.'[64] The ebullient echoes here and elsewhere of works like Kupka's *Disks* (1911–12) or Delaunay's arcs in *Electric Prism* (1914), and of Art Deco, are purely hedonistic and mark the most obvious of reconciliations with the modernist tradition. This geometric elegance and colouristic exuberance is sustained even in those square and rectangular canvasses like *Lac La Rouge II* (1968) or *River of Ponds II* (1969), or the circular *Sinjerli Variation I* (1968), which attempt to contain this protractor-generated energy. These works seem to me to represent the liberation of Stella's art from theory. His latest work, the huge aluminium reliefs of birds of 1976–7, which combine representational features and highly expressionist brushwork with geometrical experiment, confirms this development. This is a further and irretrievable move away from puritanical austerity and the theory that went with it, of a dominating logic of construction, that marked Stella's beginnings. [See Pl. 5.]

I point to Stella's modernist hedonism, since it is now the feature of his work which most eludes the clutch of critics. Stella had been dogged throughout his early career by commentators and promoters who wished to put their analyses between the beholder and the canvas. The more he insisted upon the simplicity of his painting and the immediacy of response which it demanded, the harder they tried. They thus produced pseudo-philosophical meditation on 'the nature of the object', or formal analyses of a Robbe-Grillet-like intensity and myopia.[65]

This paradoxical situation was at its worst in the case of much minimal art (of which Stella's early work was taken to be a part). The verbal miasma or aura of this kind of art had much to do with its implicit methods of procedure too, and with its being seen as making moves within the internal critical economy of art history. Suzi Gablik, for example, saw this as a sign of progress in art, away from 'iconic representation' to a logic of propositional abstract thinking about art, so that the content of the work was no longer derived from an object, but from our sense of the artist's own operations. This allowed painting 'for the first time to approach the condition of language, which is characterised by a set of generative rules'. An awful fate. In this 'language', squares, rectangles, circles, and triangles function like 'kernel sentences' in linguistics, in a 'move away from the grip of the image'.[66] (Thus for example Stella's placing of his stripes in relation to the enclosing shapes of the canvas is 'deductive'.)[67]

The analogy Miss Gablik proposes here is of course absurdly forced; it shows a minimal awareness of the complexities of actual grammatical analysis and a poor sense of the use of words like 'deductive' in logic. But it does point unerringly to the premisses, equally naïvely sustained, which inspired the producers of much minimalist art, which tended to make a very small point *via* a very simple object or series of objects, whose very banality challenges us to ask why they were as they were.[68]

It is well in accord with such assumptions for Carl André to tell us that 'what I try to find are sets of particles and the rules which combine them in the simplest way.'[69] He thus depends upon 'systematic' thinking (usually considered the antithesis of artistic thinking), as expressed in modular systems, built out of bricks, styrofoam planks, cement blocks, or wooden beams. His work is rigid, geometric, and repetitive. Only one kind of object is used in each composition. There are no adhesives or complicated joints; his works usually lie on the floor in horizontal configurations. They are frequently conceived in terms of the space available for them. The clue to our appreciation seems to depend upon our grasping the systems by which they are produced, though these are often of disarming obviousness, for example in his *Lever* (1966), which is a single line of 139 firebricks. (The exhibition in which it was shown was well entitled 'Primary Structures'.)[70] In this case however the structure André seems to have had in mind was more organic than anything else: 'All I'm doing is putting Brancusi's *Endless Column* on the ground instead of in the sky. Most sculpture is priapic with the male organ in the air. In my work, Priapus is down on the floor. The engaged position is to run along the earth.'[71]

Yet again, the interpretation has to be attached to the object by an act of critical will. And if all sculpture that sticks up, and post-André all sculpture that lies down, is phallic-Priapic, then not much has been said anyway. Although André's low-profile sculpture, of which this is an example, is reputed to have an autobiographical motive (canoeing in Summer 1965 on a New Hampshire lake, he realized that his sculpture had to be as level as water), their execution had had quite different premisses. For example, the different ways in which he has managed to lay out 120 sand lime bricks on the gallery floor, in his *Equivalents* (shown at the Tibor de Nagy Gallery in 1966). Double layers of 60 bricks each were assembled in only 4 out of 6 possible combinations: 3 times 20, 4 times 15, 6 times 10, and each combination had two versions, depending upon whether the bricks were laid on their short or their long sides. The resulting rectangular blocks were thus open to the simplest kind of mathematical inspection and offered very little to detain the eye. However, they are apparently capable of prompting some general quasi-political reflections of as broad a relevance as those of Newman cited earlier:

My work is atheistic, materialistic and communistic. It's atheistic because it's without transcendent form, without spiritual or intellectual quality. Materialistic because it's made out of its own materials without pretensions to other materials. And communistic because the form is equally accessible to all men.[72]

These naïve definitions certainly back up André's disclaimer of any intellectual quality for his work, which is sustained in his later installations with commercially available lead, magnesium, or copper plates in 12 by 12 square configurations. His mathematical demands are indeed minimal, and his availability of his materials makes much of his art accessible (i.e. repeatable) by almost anybody. Its real interest thus seems to boil down to the fact that an individual artist was able to patent these types of artistic construction for exhibition in galleries all over the world. However boring or dislikeable it may be, in its 'tough impassive anonymity' and its 'contempt for the sanctity of the art object',[73] however offensive its advertisement of its own intellectual emptiness (as if to make a vice a virtue) it at least stands as a horrible example, even if perhaps an ironic one. The fact that it boasts of its own nullity is no excuse; indeed it is a vice of much theory-dominated art, that it seems to the naïve critic to be *ipso facto* 'justifiable' however rickety the theory behind it, provided one can be devised.

In the work of Sol LeWitt, the 'underlying logic' of the work is supposed to be of equal importance to that of André, but the logic is more vigorous and the result rather more interesting: 'In conceptual art the idea or concept is the most important aspect of the work. When an artist uses a conceptual form of art, it means that all of the planning and decisions are made beforehand and that the execution is a perfunctory affair. The idea becomes a machine that makes the art.'[74] Occasionally this 'idea' is as simple as in *Lever*; for example LeWitt's *6255 lines* (1970) which is just straight short lines in rows on paper. On a more complex level, we may have a gallery filled with 'incomplete open cubes' and photographs and diagrams of them.[75] The rule that LeWitt seems to have followed here is that the resultant structure (he does not like the word 'sculpture') should be freestanding, and have enough sides (three or more) to imply a cube. Granted this, a limited series of objects can be made, with three to eleven sides of the cube. Which is demonstrated in full, in the exhibition and its accompanying book. The artist simply follows rules of construction in 'a rigid system of logic that excludes individual personality factors as much as possible'.[76] Rigid, one may feel, but hardly sophisticated, and anonymity is a peculiar virtue for an artist to aim at.

LeWitt had been working since 1966 in serial forms like this, involving systems of elementary shapes in their possible combinations. The method, so LeWitt feels, is analogous to serialism in musical composition: he was influenced to some degree by reading in 1964 an article in *Die Reihe*, which linked the work of Mallarmé to serial composition.[77] Certainly the idea of generation by ground rules,[78] without the artist's intervention, is similar. For example, in his placing five cubes in various ways upon a grid of twenty-five squares (1977), he adopted two criteria—for the first series of having the cubes with sides touching, and for the second, of having their edges touching. The books associated with these two projects reveal that there are 571 possible arrangements for the first, and 251 possible arrangements for the second series. [Cf. Pl. 6.]

LeWitt has also produced a number of very attractive-looking drawings, working usually within squares or rectangles in which are drawn tightly packed parallel lines. The rules here concern the colour of the lines (restricted to the primary red, yellow, blue, and black), their direction (vertical, horizontal, and 45° diagonals), and the order of their imposition or superimposition. He claims with some truth to produce complex results with rules which are in essence very simple. The titles of these works usually constitute an explanation of their method of generation (e.g. at its most complex, 'All single, double, triple, and quadruple combinations of lines and color in one-, two-, three- and four-part combinations' (1970)). Similarly, his wall-drawings often have their plan written beside them, 'because it aids the understanding of the idea'.[79] Such rules can be obeyed by assistants, and usually are in his later work, as for example in the wall in the Paula Cooper Gallery (1970): 'Within a six foot square, 500 vertical black lines, 500 horizontal yellow lines, 500 diagonal (left to right) blue lines, and 500 diagonal (right to left) red lines are drawn at random.'[80]

It seems that the relationship between 'idea' and result in LeWitt's work, so far as the relationship between the simple and the complex, the boring and the intriguing, the merely geometric and the complexly harmonized, is concerned, will remain a troubled one, both for the beholder and the critic. The main point that all should accept, I think, is that these works are essentially simple in idea, and that far-fetched and supposedly flattering analogies between them and 'the structural beauty of Descartes's and of Kant's treatises'[81] are as misleading as they are pretentious.

Elementary works of art like these are of course part of a long tradition; and the complexities of aesthetics and criticism have never been very good at dealing with them. And yet their function seems to have been as much to cause an abstract theoretical response in the mind, as to attract a sustained attention to an object. One has only to think of Malevich's suprematism, in particular his *White on White* of 1918, or of Josef Albers' later experiments with squares (one of the first examples of 'serial' art in American painting) or Yves Klein's single colour canvasses in *International Klein Blue*, or Robert Rauschenberg's adjoining panels of identical bare white canvas, exhibited in 1951. Even paintings of a less appealing colour, black, seem to have their own history, from Rodchenko's *Black on Black* in the Museum of Modern Art in New York, (which possibly influenced Newman's *Abraham* (1949), which is a shiny black strip over matt black, seven feet high) through Rauschenberg's textured *Black Paintings* (of 1951–2), and the extended work of Ad Reinhardt, to what seems to be, if the artist himself is to be believed, a terminal state in the work of Bob Law. Concerning his 'Ten Black Paintings', he says, grandly, that

The nature of my work can be viewed as the last complete unit picture making in western culture easel painting, the extreme of abstract expressionism. So much so that one is no longer looking at paint but one is forced to be aware of an idea of a painting idea. At this point one has entered into conceptual art and my work is the transition from pictures on the wall to conceptual art in the head.[82]

The black painting is thus one of the simplest of single art objects. Its significance has to come either from its ability to empty the mind in contemplation (or to fill it with stunned irrelevancies) or from its critical context. And of course the critical point may be quite simple: we expect a painting to be an image of some kind: these are not. The point can be dramatically extended, as it was in the Bob Law exhibition, by filling a huge room with black paintings. Here the frustration of expectation is compounded, but a further dimension is added. It is not just the function of the painting that is called in question: but also that of the Gallery, which is both finessing on its own function of showing paintings (images) and also constructing a large minimalist work of art, by spacing the black paintings on its walls. It thus becomes a kind of conceptual art radically different from that of André and LeWitt; for it involves dramatic surprise and critical paradox, rather than theoretical elaboration.

Indeed by about 1970, Bob Law's way of thinking about art 'in the head' had already become very popular among a large school of relatively minor conceptual artists. Even the black painting idea could be put to use, it seems, in Mel Ramsden's *Secret Painting* (1967–8), whose conceptual pretensions are made critically explicit by the statement which is to be hung beside it:

> The content of this painting is invisible; the character and dimensions of the contents are to be kept permanently secret, known only to the artist.

The 'idea' of a picture is called into question: as it is also in Ian Burns's *Mirror Piece* (1967) which also raised the Duchampian question (first posed by his ready-mades) concerning what sorts of objects we are willing to treat (as if they were) works of art. ('Can this be thought of/made a work of art by being thought of/intended to be one?') Burns, too, makes his intentions tediously clear with an accompanying text, which explains that a mirror in a room is recognized as such through its normal function, that a mirror in a gallery is assumed to be intended as art, and thirdly that the same mirror hanging in a gallery displayed with notes and diagrams (as is Burns's) is a step further, because (to quote from one of Burns's own notes) 'The concept becomes a framework for the mirror *as art* and aims at getting the spectator's "seeing" to cohere against a particular background of inferred knowledge. The context of room or gallery no longer serves to identify the function of the mirror; the intention is built into the work.' These black and mirror pictures tell us what we already know; they thus seem less individual in conception, and lack the surprise that goes with wit to be found in other critical games with our preconceptions concerning art, like Terry Atkinson and Michael Baldwin's *Map* (1967) which simply displays the outlines of the states of Iowa and Kentucky in their correct relative positions, and, as is obligingly pointed out in the accompanying text, leaves out the rest of the map of North-East America. Indeed art of this kind seems to me to work best as a kind of Zen joke: it so often has so small or clumsy a critical point to make, that it helps to have it accompanied by a small amount of amusement. (Though occasionally one is unsure whether a given work in this style is presented ironically or is merely obsessively boring, as for example On Kanara's *One Million Years* (1970), which is column after column of numbers.)

This type of conceptual art thus earns its label in so far as it depends upon intellectual ingenuity; the aim is to get the point, rather than to enjoy the object or activity involved. This often depends upon a kind of inspired arbitrariness, as in Denis Oppenheim's *Energy Displacement—approaching Theatricality* (1970), performed by the art department of the University of Wisconsin at Whitewater. Here, a race was held in a swimming-pool, the relative positions of the competitors recorded as the winner touched the end of the bath, and then mapped on to a plan of the stalls of the Ambassador Theatre in New York. The competitors were then given appropriate tickets for the theatre, the winner's being closest to the stage. Here the activity depends, as art, purely upon its documentation (a photograph of the race and an inscribed theatre plan).[83] It is indeed typical of much conceptual art that it basically documents activities which, performed by 'artists', supposedly for an artistic 'purpose', are presumed to have an artistic 'effect'.

One might cite as an example, Jan Dibbets's postcards, recording a place (photographed), a gesture (thumbs up, also photographed), and the artist's intention (in four languages) to perform the gesture photographed in the place photographed at a particular time. Less inventive perhaps is On Kanara once more, who obviously likes doing things again and again with small variations, and so capitalized on the need for nightly sleep by informing the art critic Ursula Meyer by postcard from Japan of the time he got up in the morning. (For what it is worth, between 25th and 28th November 1970, he got up at 8.03 a.m., 8.26 a.m., 8.34 a.m., and 8.01 a.m.)

The primary function of such artists is to provide us with information; and it is not particularly clear on what basis the information is selected, nor on what basis the 'artists' are recognized as such by providing it. It is perhaps this aspect of their activities that has allowed the conceptualists to be seen as an anti-bourgeois, egalitarian school confronting the 'gallery-museum complex': to each man or woman his artistic 'idea'. Even so, we are left with the museum, the art book, and the art critic, as the essential loci, and longer-term preservers, of the artistic activity: as Siegelaub remarked, 'When information is PRIMARY, the catalogue can become the exhibition.'

But there is a question that still nags—can the theory of art be made artistically interesting? Not I think when it is trivial or boring, as in LeWitt's *6255 lines*, but certainly when it is allied to some more traditional artistic and psychological value, like humour or irony. (This the surrealists and dadaists well knew.) What is more, for success, the critical point has to be reinforced by a real disturbance in the audience's expectations, and not one that can be simply shrugged off, or accepted by making an equally minimalist logical connection in the mind. That is why perhaps the most successful conceptual art has been the most dramatic. It is to be found outside the plastic arts, as well. Thus Beckett's *Breath* (1969), a minimalist play if ever there was one, calls into question our notions of dramatic performance, confronting us as it does with a pile of rubbish ('no verticals', though), an increase and decrease of lighting, two identical cries ('Instant of recorded vagitus'), and an amplified recording of breathing.

Similarly defeating is John Cage's notorious *4' 33" (tacet) for any instruments* (1952), a musical version of Ramsden's secret painting and Burns's mirror combined, for in it both nothing (silence) and everything reflected back on the audience (the noise in the concert hall) happens. The first performance of *4' 33"* took place in August 1952 in the Maverick Concert Hall, in Woodstock, New York. In it a pianist enters, sits at the piano for four minutes and thirty-three seconds, but does not play. The piece was originally in three movements, signified by the performer's moving his arms, but this was later dropped. The 'music' is simply the accidental noises in the room in which the piece is 'performed'. The score is in Peters's catalogue, number 6777. Here the concert hall, as the gallery for visual art, is relied upon to control our attention in a particular way. Until you know what *4' 33"* is as a 'piece of music', you could be really let down by it. Now that everyone knows, I suppose that the piece also exists as a piece of verbal description. It did, once, startle its audience into considering the notion of performance. What was the point at which they realized that the pianist was not just waiting to perform, but actually performing? It made its critical point. But once that point has been made, little of any value may remain.

Chapter Three: I. Time Suspended

'There is not enough seriousness in what we do,' Kevin said. 'Everyone wanders around having his own individual perceptions. These, like balls of different colours and shapes and sizes, roll around on the green billiard table of consciousness . . .' Kevin stopped and began again. 'Where is the figure in the carpet? Or is it just . . . carpet?' he asked. 'Where is——' 'You're talking a lot of buffalo hump, you know that,' Hubert said.
Donald Barthelme, *Snow White*.

In this chapter I shall discuss works in which, for one reason or another, any pretence at linear logical development to a conclusion is modified or discarded, so that one of the most usual conventions for intelligibility may be knocked away. By a 'logical' procedure I mean in this context one which allows for the question why one element is related to another (or, more usually, succeeds another) to have an intelligible answer. Examples of this are the succession of events within a plot, or succession of chords within the tonal system, or the relationship between areas of a painting as licensed by some reference to an object imitated, or some formal criterion of symmetry or design. All the works discussed in the previous chapter have this form of logical development, though as we have seen, the conventions for their use have often been radically altered. On the other hand works which discard such procedures may be in extreme cases internally self-contradictory, self-cancelling, or self-destructive.

I shall distinguish three main possibilities here: firstly, those works which don't seem to their audience to 'get anywhere', but which are nevertheless held together by some kind of background convention, secondly, those in which the elements are juxtaposed in a collage technique that does not allow for the conventional types of thematic relationship, and finally, those in which any such 'logical' relationship between elements is in any case deliberately precluded by chance (aleatoric) procedures of composition.

I

Our discussion of serial works in the previous chapter reminded us that music has traditionally depended upon implicative relationships. Thus we feel the slow introduction of a symphony leading us by modulation into the statement of its first subject, or the slow rise to the dominant seventh and its resolution in *Tristan and Isolde*, or the movement of the music by rhythmic means even in a work in twelve-note style, like Stravinsky's *Agon*. Indeed Schoenberg's own work, by retaining such traditional rhythmic procedures, has a perpetually striving sense of forward movement, yet one which is deprived of the usual harmonic goals. It is this deprivation which gives it much of its expressionist, almost hysterical effect.

This sense of periodicity and pulse has always helped to define music as the time-dominated sequential art *par excellence*. The ways in which it has been characterized have of course varied from period to period, and may in many ways be taken to reflect cultural values—from the comparative smoothness and control of Mozart to the barbaric rhythms of *The Rite of Spring*. In the postmodern period however, we have a music whose changing sequence of events may depend upon no such rhythmic drive, goals, or points of culmination. In the most extreme cases it is simply *there*, between stopping and starting. In others, the suspension of movement may have a quite specific psychological or even religious point.

Thus the music is almost in a state of suspended animation in Messiaen's *Vingt regards sur l'enfant Jésus* where reiterated figuration produces a music virtually without movement. (Similar effects had been produced by Satie and Debussy.) It has been argued that our western time-sense is simply irrelevant to such music, and that it recreates modes of sensibility from other cultures in which the time-sense is very different (for example of the Gothic motet, or of Indian improvisation).[1] This seems to be a very good way of seeing the matter; for the use of eastern melismatic devices, or the almost stationary alternation of two or three chromatic chords, or the slow build-up of purely 'atmospheric' sounds as in Ligeti's *Lontano*, demands a quite different response from the listener from that to classical or nineteenth-century music. We must give up our normal expectations, in order to participate in a quite different kind of experience. We have to accept the moment in and for itself. This is, once more, foreshadowed in Debussy, though with him the method is often related to some kind of extra-musical impressionism. The general effect is to make music an abstract art of the contemplative moment, like abstract painting, though demanding (as some of Rothko's paintings do) a ritualistic time-scale. It can be a peculiarily will-less kind of art, in which the decision and energy of developmental temporal relationships is dissipated, and the succession of timbres and sonorities is as important as any development of theme.

This analogy between music and abstract visual pattern particularly inspired Messiaen, as we have already seen. Colour and timbre dominate the thematic; new sounds combine as new colours. We pay attention to momentary aspects of sound quality, as we do to colour quality, and the relationships between them can be as unpredictable as the relationships between shapes and abstract painting. Conventional organizing forms are discarded in favour of a much more intuitive placing of elements. Thus Messiaen says that 'certaines sonorités sont liées pour moi à certains complexes de couleurs et je les utilise comme des couleurs, en les juxtaposant et en les mettant en valeur les unes par les autres, comme un peintre souligne une couleur par sa complémentaire'.[2] Thus the form of his *Couleurs de la cité céleste* (1963) 'depends entirely upon colours, and the melodic and rhythmic themes, the combinations of sounds and timbres, change in the manner of colours'.[3] The players are even instructed in the score to play red, and so on. The external inspiration for this procedure comes from passages in the *Apocalypse* (a text suggested to Messiaen by the sonority of the trombones specified in the original commission).

Messiaen's method here, and elsewhere, involves a crucial matter of aesthetic principle, and one which applies to many postmodern works. This is, that our reaction to the sounds of such a work needs to be as little directed as it would be in looking at an abstract painting. We have to accept them simply as they are and as they occur (like a light show) though the analogy for the Messiaen would more appropriately be stained glass. We enjoy them for themselves, without allowing too many underlying expectations as to what will happen next to interfere. The primacy of immediate sense-experience is asserted—we must hear a chord, for example, not as if it is related to what follows, but 'for itself'; confirming Stravinsky's dictum that 'Harmony, considered as a doctrine dealing with chords and chord relations, has had a brilliant but short history.'[4] The method is anti-hierarchical in its obliteration of causal pattern, and is typical of our period. Thus in the novel, phenomenalistic observation and presentation supplants explanation; no event need presume or imply the existence of any other event, and the same principle may apply to marks on canvas as much as to sounds. These techniques are of course extreme ones, and we will see them at their fullest extension when we come to discuss aleatoric works. But the underlying assumption here is, very frequently, that we should not understand events by grasping their function; what is aimed at is a passive and non-selective sensing. A consequence of this is that the critic tends to be forced into (merely) descriptive rather than analytic or interpretative roles (as I shall be in much of what follows) since the work contains no significant hierarchy of structure. The value chiefly subserved is surprise or novelty. Hence the astounding inventiveness of many modern composers in terms of orchestration and sonority, and the tendency of critics to praise avant-garde works above all for their creation of unique 'sound worlds', as recognizable for their colouring and style as the work of abstract painters.

Although it in fact has a strict serialist organization, Boulez's *Le Marteau sans maître* (first performed at the ISCM in June 1955) is a key work in the development of post-war music for these very reasons. As did Schoenberg's *Pierrot Lunaire* in the modernist period, it creates an absolutely distinctive sound picture, cut loose from all previously accepted associative links. It is a work which to some degree breaks away from Boulez's earlier method of composition; it is 'un premier pas vers une brisure effective de la continuité musicale' ('an important stage in my progress towards what was effectively the breaking up of musical continuity')[5] and is thus a reply to his own *Structures 1a*. It is an immensely evocative work whose percussive rhythms recall Stravinsky, and whose athematicism and balancing of sound and silence recall Webern. In it a surrealist text by René Char, itself released from logically ordered thinking processes, is set to the most disembodied of musical accompaniments, for alto flute, viola, vibraphone, guitar, and extended percussion. Rhythms are disintegrated beyond the point at which they can be 'grouped' by the listener (as they still can in Webern). Often enough the players are working to different rhythmic pulses anyway. Pitch is of little importance (parly because all parameters are serialized) and timbre and sonority are all. Although the music pulsates with tension on the small scale or in the individual part, these tensions cancel one another out, so that the effect of the music is curiously floating and static. Boulez's infinitely inventive figuration passes by at such a speed that our sense of temporal progression is paradoxically slowed down. As he points out, 'Si l'on incorpore dans une structure de rhythmes assez simples, des accumulations de petites notes qui font que le tempo est brisé à chaque moment, on perd complètement la notion de vitesse.'[6] Any notion of consonance or dissonance is entirely irrelevant. This is delicate, tender, melismatic, and nervous music, which is devoted to our sense of flux, from which at the same time it releases us. It is 'une musique qui peut se passer complètement de pulsations; une musique qui flotte' ('a kind of music that can do entirely without pulsations—a music that seems to float').[7]

My description of the effect of this piece is (I hope) confirmed by the comments of Stravinsky, whose ear can hardly be faulted. He is denying that one can relate the notes of *Le Marteau* tonally, that there may be such a hierarchizing key to this kind of work:

. . . all that the ear can be aware of in this sense is density. . . . And density has become a strict serial matter, an element for variation and permutation like any other; according to one's system one gets from two to twelve notes in vertical aggregation . . . All of this goes back to Webern . . . with a piece like 'après l'artisanat furieux' [the third movement] however, one follows the lines of only a single instrument and is content to be 'aware of' the others. Perhaps later the second line and the third will be familiar, but one mustn't try to hear them in the tonal-harmonic sense.[8]

Many of the characteristics described above are enduring ones for Boulez's music, and they can have some severe disadvantages for the listener. The problem is precisely the one pointed to by Stravinsky: for much postmodern music there are no agreed harmonic backgrounds, even within the context of serialism. Since Boulez cannot give us the structural sense of such a background, against which to foreground his own procedures, then as Hans Keller points out 'What his music lacks is any sense of harmonic *movement*, with the result that from a vertical point of view we are often presented with a catalogue of sonorities, rather than a continuous evolution of vertical tensions and distensions.'[9] Thus even his work on a large scale, like *Pli selon pli*, for soprano and large orchestra, to a text by Mallarmé, in which one might expect some clear structural articulation, although it 'glitters and gleams' is ultimately both 'narcissistic and stagnant', a floating through harmonic chaos.[10] In the end, or long before it, we have that overloading effect which I suggested earlier was characteristic of much postmodern art. The catalogue of sonorities, like a long sequence of *Finnegans Wake* polysemy, becomes fatiguing. This effect relates very closely to Boulez's choice of text: 'Ce qui m'a séduit chez Mallarmé . . . c'est l'extraordinaire densité formelle de ses poèmes . . . jamais la langue française n'a été menée aussi loin du point de vue de la syntaxe.' This is a complexity for which Boulez felt driven to provide a musical equivalent, which was chiefly concerned with sonority and with structures to mirror Mallarmé's rhyme-schemes.[11] Yet music like this seems to need a smaller Webernian scale to avoid destroying itself as it proceeds. Although the experience may be intended to be one of mystical, *Four Quartets*-like insight, these are not surrounded by that more discursive argument that serves to give such insights value. The common or mundane, the expressive or emotional, is banished, and we are left with no sense of scale by which to measure the experience.

Boulez's work thus has an apparent discontinuity of effect and lack of forward movement despite its often rigorous underlying serialist plan. But a wholly *explicit* aesthetic of discontinuity is found in a number of works by Stockhausen, produced late in the 1950s, which even more deliberately concentrate upon the individual moment. Thus he says of his *Kontakte* (a work which exists in two versions; for electronic sounds, and for the electronic sounds plus piano and percussion, dating from 1959–60) that

The work is composed in 'moment form'. Each moment, whether a state or a process, is individual and self-regulated, and able to sustain an independent existence. The musical events do not take a fixed course between a determined beginning and an inevitable ending, and the moments are not merely consequents of what precedes them and antecedents of what follows; rather the concentration on the Now—on every Now—as if it were a vertical slice dominating over any horizontal conception of time and reaching into timelessness, which I call eternity: an eternity which does not begin at the end of time, but is attainable at every *moment*.[12]

One may of course doubt the efficacy of this Blakean attempt to 'Hold Infinity in the palm of your hand/And eternity in an Hour' ('Auguries of Innocence'). Stockhausen frequently makes such pretentious metaphysical claims. But the work leaves the listener free in the way he specifies; and in the version for electronics and piano there is an interaction between the two musical modes which is most successful, as one type of sound 'comments' on the other.

His *Carré*, for four orchestras and four choirs, which he also wrote in 1959–60, has a similar aesthetic: 'This piece tells no story. You can confidently stop listening for a moment if you cannot or do not want to go on listening; for each moment can stand on its own and at the same time is related to all the other moments.'[13] The composer's comment here comes, significantly enough, after a quotation from Beckett's *The Unnameable*. The music (in the severely edited recording) frequently breaks off into silence, emphasizing a discontinuity which is in any case very disturbing to the listener. Any adjustment we might try to make to the extraordinary succession of sounds devised by Stockhausen and his assistant for this work, Cornelius Cardew, is perpetually overturned by a new episode. Robin Maconie, who is one of the most acute commentators on Stockhausen's music, is interestingly enough forced to use a number of discrete images of motion to describe the effect of these episodes:

Sounds pass by in a flash, or they overtake in slow motion, and these external events encroach upon long, sustained constant tones, which signify both our motionlessness *and* our being moved—sounds representing, that is, the whine of a motor. All these images appear in *Carré*, and the same indirect associations between disparate elements may be heard to apply: the relationship of a sustained pitch (moving at constant speed) to the intensity of inner activity of opposing (overtaking) blocks of sound, or the sharpness and 'speed' of staccato chords (sounds moving in an opposite direction), or to the relationship between distance and rate of change.[14]

This stereophonically moving and dramatically changing music is thus described rather in the way in which one might describe the changes in sound and movement of a large amount of traffic; and this image seems to me to be a fair approximation to the effect not only of this, but of many later electronic works. *Carré* had a great influence upon later composers, like Ligeti and Penderecki, whose work, like this one, can be wholly athematic, and concentrate entirely upon textures. Ligeti in particular has produced some immensely impressive orchestral works, like *Atmosphères* (1961) and *Lontano* (1967) which sustain this new musical impressionism with sounds which always seems as precisely *heard* by the composer and hence by the listener, as any by earlier composers. Where Stockhausen's work sometimes seems synthesized and extravagantly complex, that of Ligeti leaves the impression that no detail is irrelevant.

However one of the most remarkable, and to my mind successful, of those works which suspend our normal time-sense, is Stockhausen's own *Stimmung* (Tuning) of 1968. This is partly because the composer does here retain a background convention to unify the whole, to guarantee a basic continuity and intelligibility against which his rhythmic and verbal procedures, some of them aleatoric, can be maintained. Thus for the full 73 minutes (of the recording) *Stimmung* is based upon the natural harmonics of a low B fundamental, of which the vocalists sing the 2nd, 3rd, 4th, 6th, 7th, and 9th overtones. The timbres of these overtones are varied, and notated precisely according to the international phonetic alphabet. The course of the piece depends upon the singer's free decision. They each have 8 or 9 'models' and 11 'magic names' which, following the formal schema, they can bring into play freely according to the context, and to which the other singers may react with 'transformations', 'varied deviation', 'beats', and 'identity'. The model-following singer always takes the lead but can relinquish it when he wishes. And once a magic name has been 'called' as the choice of a singer, it is 'repeated periodically in the tempo, and with approximately the same articulation as the model till renewed identity is achieved, and is thus integrated into the prevalent model'.[15] Thus the surprising or unanticipated event is blended into the underlying texture, with a beautifully calming and yet precise emotional effect, for this good tuning, or 'being together' is supposed to lead to a 'standing still and vibrating inside . . . like a butterfly sitting on a blossom'. The whole has a ritual feeling like the singing of Tibetan monks: 'Certainly *Stimmung* is meditative music. Time is suspended. One listens to the inner self of the sound, the inner self of the harmonic spectrum, the inner self of the vowel, the INNER SELF. Subtlest fluctuations, scarcely a ripple. In the beauty of the sensual shines the beauty of the eternal.'[16]

I am very struck by the formal similarity between *Stimmung* and Beckett's *Play* (first performed in 1963, in Germany, and the following year in London) in which the introduction of new phrases and dramatic incidents is also perpetually brought back to a central situation (the eternal triangle of adultery) amongst its players, which corresponds to Stockhausen's central chord. Indeed the over-all organization of *Play* is itself musical, with its obsessive returns to central themes, and its repeated sentences. Its three speakers are like the circle of singers of *Stimmung* in another respect; for they do not move, being imprisoned in urns. The spotlight which moves among them and, like the baton of a hidden conductor, makes them speak, also corresponds in its seeming unpredictability to the random initiation of phrases in *Stimmung* by its singers. (One might compare the use of the baton in Beckett's *Words and Music*.) Both works too suspend time; though menacingly so in *Play*, for its two women and a man, in their hell-like situation, reminiscent of Sartre's *Huis-clos*, seem condemned to an eternal return as they repeat the text for a second time. Where Stockhausen is concerned with contemplative hedonism, Beckett concentrates fiercely upon psychological pain. His characters, like those of Yeats's Noh plays, are destined to dream back through their past lives, and like those of his *Purgatory*, they are forced to stay at a moment of crisis, of emotional impasse.

Thus *Play* opens with all the speakers, Woman 1, Woman 2, and Man, all speaking simultaneously for some while; there is a pause, and then a 'chord'

Woman 1:		I said to him, give her up—
Woman 2:	together	One morning as I was sitting—
Man:		We were not long together—

which keys in the following speeches, till the next chord, when the spotlights go to half-strength. Each speaker seems to be unaware of the others, trapped in a monologue which centres round a number of repeated sentences or phrases, provoked by the basic situation. Thus for example,

Woman 2: One morning as I was sitting by the open window . . . what are you talking about? I said, stitching away . . . I was doing my nails, by the open window.

And this is later echoed:

Woman 1: Perhaps she is sitting somewhere, by the open window, her hands folded in her lap, gazing down on the olives.

As the last quotation suggests, they are bound together in a perpetual counterpoint of phrases, which obsessively recall their common past situation:

Woman 1: I said to him, give her up . . . .

Woman 2: Give him up she screamed, he's mine . . . .
Man: Give up that whore, she said, or I'll cut my throat—(*hiccup*)—pardon—so help me God.

Play ends as the opening chord comes round for the third time. The whole is curiously unlifelike—with that essential separation between the performers characteristic of musical performance, in which the players co-operate but are essentially separate part players, their work co-ordinated from outside by a conductor or leader. In *Play*, as in *Stimmung*, the themes for discussion are announced by the players in turn. The whole has the inevitability, the sense of a lack of freedom of manœuvre, and the exact pacing (shown in Beckett's stage directions for the pauses in speech and the uses of the spotlight) of musical performance. This is indeed what *Play* essentially is, as George Devine noted, from a director's point of view: '. . . one has to think of the text as something like a musical score wherein the "notes", the sights, the sounds, the pauses, have their own special interrelated rhythms, and out of their composition comes the dramatic impact.'[17]

Beckett's work has very frequently been based upon this kind of remorseless thematic logic which, in the end, seems baffling or self-destructive, and ends in stasis. This has been so from *Watt* on, with its page after page of minute logical alternatives, and its incidents which are, as the narrator himself remarks, 'of great formal brilliance and indeterminable import',[18] like suspended chords. Hesitation goes hand in hand with precision; perpetual qualification gives the reader the sense of getting nowhere, being as trapped in Beckett's prose as Watt is in Mr Knott's house, or Malone is in bed. Some stay against confusion is indeed provided by incidental jokes, but these do not prevent us from stepping back from his Shandyesque plots, or even the profundity of his philosophical reflections, and asking what the point of their relation to such extreme tortuosities of style may be. Perhaps its underlying motive is partly revealed in Beckett's famous statement of 1949 in his dialogue with Georges Duthuit: 'There is nothing to express, nothing with which to express, nothing from which to express, together with the obligation to express.'[19] Or, in the concluding words from *The Unnameable*: 'you must go on, I can't go on, I'll go on'. In this novel, and the trilogy as a whole, the style fully expresses the near-nihilism of the underlying attitude:

I invented it all, in the hope it would console me, help me to go on, allow myself to think of myself as somewhere in a road, moving, between a beginning and an end, gaining ground, losing ground, getting lost, but somehow in the long run making headway. All lies. I have nothing to do, that is to say nothing in particular. I have to speak, whatever that means. Having nothing to speak. No one compels me to, there is no one, it's an accident, a fact. Nothing can ever exempt me from it.[20]

Thought becomes language, which itself offers a terrain for an exploration which is nevertheless far removed from the play of other writers. For Beckett's work projects images of an absurd existence which is as entrammelling and as inexorable as his own mode of expression.

Indeed what is particularly interesting is the way in which such stoical philosophical attitudes are not only explicitly stated, but also gain formal expression, in his later, more experimental period, which seems to me to have advanced from modernist Joycean monologue, to distinctively postmodern methods of procedure. *Comment c'est* (1961) for example is a serialist work in its over-all statement (like the *nouveau roman* the book uses the repeated but varied sentence as one of its main building units). It is also minimalist and 'moment'-like in its parts—unpunctuated paragraphs divided by white space, spasmodic attempts at expression lost in a chaos or eternity of time. As in *Play*, the basic structure tends to an inferno-like repetition both of the literary form and of the torment associated with it, bound upon a Dantesque circle (hence the pun on 'comment c'est' (commencez) at the very end of the book).

The plot, such as it is, is simple, tripartite, and announced in the opening sentence—before Pim, with Pim, and after Pim: 'comment c'était je cite avant Pim avec Pim après Pim comment c'est trois parties je le dis comme je l'entends'.[21]

The narrator is face down in mud (or excrement) in a world of darkness, through which he drags himself painfully for ever and ever, 10 or 15 yards at a time, pulling after him a sack full of supplies—tins of tunny fish (reminiscent of *Caliban upon Setebos*) and a tin-opener—the sack tied at the mouth by a rope which is attached to his neck: 'le sac quand il sera vide mon sac une possession ce mot qui siffle tout bas ici une possession bref abîme et apposition enfin anomalie anomalie un sac ici mon sac quand il sera vide bah j'ai le temps des siècles'.[22]

The relationship between narrator and deuteragonist (Pim) which dominates the second part, is essentially that between sadist and victim, exploited with similarly grim humour elsewhere in Beckett, notably in *Godot* and *End Game*:

tableau des excitations de base un chante ongles dans l'aisselle deux parle fer de l'ouvre-boîte dans le cul trois stop coup de poing sur le crâne quatre plus fort manche de l'ouvre-boîte dans le rein cinq moins fort index dans l'anus six bravo claque à cheval sur les fesses sept mauvais même que trois huit encore même que un ou deux selon[23]

In part three of the book the narrator realizes he is not alone; he, it seems, is in turn awaiting Bom, who will treat him as he has treated Pim. The situation thus repeats itself endlessly, without beginning or end: 'et ces mêmes couples qui éternellement se reconstituent d'un bout à l'autre de cette immense procession que c'est toujours à la millionième fois ça se laisse concevoir comme à l'inconcévable première deux étrangers qui s'unissent pour les besoins du tourment'.[24] And this torment can only be coped with, as elsewhere in Beckett, by page after page of calculation, by a determined rationalism as opposed to chaos, as the narrator assigns a number to each of the million victims, and imagines their means of communication along the line. Yet nothing is learnt: the novel turns in upon itself—it can be read from any point on, it perpetually refers to its own three parts, to notes and to a book which may be that of Judgement, and it even incorporates a criticism of its own speaking—'que peut on bien se dire dans ces moments-là', 'c'est vite dit une fois trouvé', 'tout ça je le dis comme je l'entends', 'quelque chose-là qui ne va pas': 'Dieu sait si je suis souvent heureux mais jamais plus jamais autant qu'à cet instant-là bonheur malheur je sais je sais mais on peut en causer.'[25] We are uncertain even of the status of the narrator with respect to his 'world' for a good part of the time; it is uncertain whether an anonymous narrator or Pim is speaking, since they are both perhaps called Pim, or whether Bom is remembering, or whether the narrator is simply losing the sense of his own identity.[26] There is thus a basic indeterminacy at the heart of the work, a lack of any sense of stable relationships, despite the repetition. The events in the baroque hotel of *L'Année dernière à Marienbad* have turned from love to hate and been moved to Hell. Indeed in a Robbe-Grillet-like act of *gommage*, it is suddenly asserted that the whole story is false:

si tout ça tout ça oui si tout ça n'est pas comment dire pas de réponse si tout ça n'est pas faux oui
tous ces calculs oui explications oui toute l'histoire d'un bout à l'autre oui complètement faux oui[27]

Comment c'est is thus a startling extension of that new view of literature which was foreseen by Sartre in introducing one of the earliest of new novels: 'Les anti-romans conservent l'apparence et les contours du roman . . . Mais c'est pour mieux décevoir; il s'agit de contester le roman par lui-même, de la détruire sous nos yeux dans le temps qu'on semble l'édifier.'[28] But it is Beckett's supreme achievement, paralleling that of Borges noted earlier, to take an experimental technique and use it, not to play a game which perpetually refers back to the author's own procedures or language, but to create an imaginary world and a structure for it whose halting suspension in time revives for us one of the most terrifying and yet traditional images of the human condition: that of Hell on earth.

Chapter Three: II. The Disordered Environment: Collage

We have so far discussed art which may suspend our normal expectations concerning temporal progression (by harmonic implication or narrative change) but which nevertheless has a potentially discernible underlying logic of construction. We now approach works in which any such logic may be discarded, whose aesthetic is one of deliberate discontinuity, often playful and dadaist. All our usual critical assumptions about the unity of the work are called into question, and may have to be cast aside. Some of the works we shall be concerned with refuse *any* univocal meaning: their only ideology (supposedly) is the refusal of restrictively organizing conventions of production and interpretation.

I

In modernism, the unity of the literary work seemed similarly to be threatened, not only by occasional ideological incoherence (as in Pound's *Cantos* and Auden's *The Orators*) but also very frequently by the use of a collage technique of juxtaposition, rather than of narrative or logical sequence. Thus critics are still uncertain how or even whether *The Waste Land* really holds together, even if one can point to a number of thematic and psychological binding factors. Even so, the whole bent of modernist symbol-seeking and mythopoeic criticism has been to attempt to construct a unity and coherence for the works it analyses. The challenge to the critic to seek out a binding theme is a familiar one. In many postmodernist works however, those binding conventions which in modernism made the parts of a collage seem to behave like the disjointed terms of a metaphor, with an unstated thematic linking, are often even harder to find. Carlos Williams's *Paterson*, for example, is a kind of rag-bag city epic, incorporating heterogeneous chunks of language like Duchampian 'ready-mades' (in descent from Dos Passos's *USA* trilogy). It is a work which makes us feel that its parts are found and juxtaposed; that they are exemplars, rather than stages within an implicit argument,—even one conducted upon a symbolic level. As Jonathan Raban has pointed out, its snippets of conversation, history, and gossip reflect the idea that the form a poem takes must itself imitate the discontinuity, the contingency, and the disjunctive social patterns of life in an industrial society.[29]

These assumptions are most ambitiously tested in Michel Butor's prose-poem *Mobile: étude pour une représentation des États-Unis* (1962). This work has fifty 'chapters', one for each state taken in alphabetic order, and a time-scheme of forty-eight hours over the spring equinox. Thus the sections for the 'daylight' states begin with a 'Welcome to —— ' road sign, which is omitted at 'night' because the fictional traveller would not be able to see it from his car. But this structure yields nothing like a plot and certainly does not reflect any one possible journey across America. It merely affects the state headings and the descriptions of times of day (or nocturnal dreams) which are embedded in a mass of extraneous matter. For in writing *Mobile* Butor deliberately abandoned the closely organized linear narrative of his earlier novels to produce a text with no finally decided, closed or finished form. The reader encounters an elaborately ambiguous Mallarméan typographical arrangement of fragments. Thus there are five depths of margin, so that the leftmost may concern the state whose chapter it is, and the others neighbouring states progressively more removed from it. Hundreds of place-names, kinds of ice cream whose colours are echoed in descriptions of cars, miscellaneous historical and tourist information, people saying 'Hello', descriptions of Indian and Negro culture, names of plants, birds, trees, fragments of advertising copy, newspaper reports, political statements, weather reports, extracts from the Salem witch trials, commendations of 'Freedomland', prospectuses for medical books, lists of film stars, titles of songs by Elvis Presley, and so on, jostle together on the page. The basic syntactic form is the list, echoing that of the sales catalogue, quotations from which also have a large part to play in the text and seem to symbolize American consumerism and diversity. Many formulae recur: one which implicitly reflects the journeying movement of the whole is that in which we have the sequence make of car—its colour—the colour of its driver—and of his shirt—and the names of the

1. Jackson Pollock, *The She-Wolf*, 1943; oil, gouache, and plaster on canvas, 41⅞ × 67 in. Collection, The Museum of Modern Art, New York

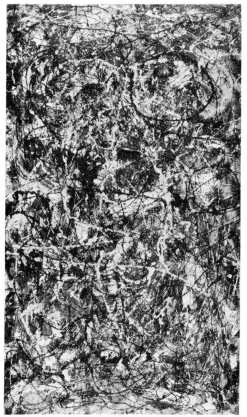

2. Jackson Pollock, *Full Fathom Five*, 1947; oil on canvas with nails, tacks, buttons, key, coins, cigarettes, matches, etc., 50⅞ × 30⅛ in. Collection, The Museum of Modern Art, New York. Gift of Peggy Guggenheim

3. Barnett Newmann, *Adam*, 1951–2; oil on canvas, $95\frac{5}{8} \times 79\frac{7}{8}$ in.

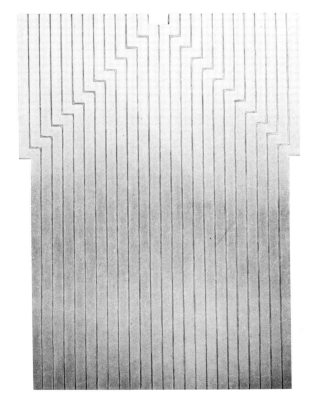

5. Frank Stella, *Tahkt-I-Sulayman I*, 1967; polymer and fluorescent polymer paint on canvas, 120¼ × 242¼ in.

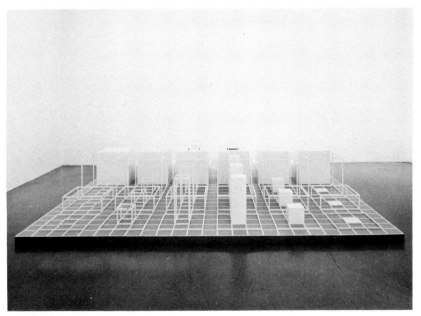

6. Sol LeWitt, *Serial Project No. 1 (ABCD)*, 1966; baked enamel on aluminium, 20 in. × 13 ft. 7 in. Collection, The Museum of Modern Art, New York

4 *(left)*. Frank Stella, *Luis Miguel Dominguin*, 1960; aluminium paint on canvas, 96 × 72 in.

8. Robert Rauschenberg, *Untitled*, 1955; collage on canvas, $15\frac{1}{2} \times 20\frac{3}{4}$ in.

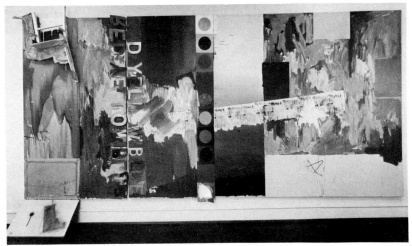

9. Jasper Johns, *According to What*, 1964; oil on canvas with objects, 88 × 192 in.

7 *(left)*. Robert Rauschenberg, *Crocus*, 1962; oil on canvas, 60 × 36 in.

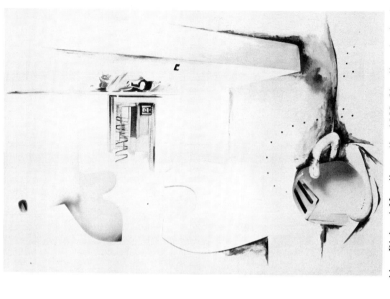

11. Richard Hamilton, *She*, 1958–61; oil and mixed media on board, 48 × 32 in.

10. Peter Blake, *On the Balcony*, 1955–7; oil on canvas, 47¾ × 35¾ in.

12. Claes Oldenburg, *Bedroom Ensemble I*, 1963

13. Tom Wesselmann, *Great American Nude No. 54*, 1964; mixed media, 7 ft. × 8½ ft. × 39 in.

14. Mark Rothko, *Black on Maroon*, 1958; oil on canvas, 105 × 144 in.

lakes, mountains, or rivers past which, presumably, he drives.

The pages of this book-as-object are thus like the parts of a mobile. Their typographical parts reveal new aspects as they are repeated with variations, and they can be moved back and forth at will (unlike film or tape) and thus offer a number of 'routes' through this representation of a country. Like America itself it is decentred, and full of cultural and ideological and geographical gaps reflecting tensions within the culture. This is in spite of its occasional and ironic references to Washington as a Mecca-like religious centre: 'la pratique religieuse la plus importante des Européens d'Amérique est le pélérinage à la ville sacrée de Washington, où se trouvent les principaux temples et les organes essentiels du gouvernement'.[30]

A fascinating tension is thus set up between the fragmentation of any particular sequence (this supposedly representing the discontinuity of reality and the way in which we are daily bombarded from all sides by information whose truth or falsity we cannot possibly assess)[31] and our growing awareness that the fragments do fall into thematic groups and thus implicitly at least encourage us to make judgements. Presumably the prejudices of author and reader are meant to coincide when the many quotations from Sears and Montgomery Ward catalogues are taken to reflect an abundance of consumer choice (paradoxically enough reflected in the freedom of choice which this mode of writing offers). It would be conventional to believe that the first of these is bad and the second good. Even more importantly, one cannot fail to notice that there are many descriptions of Indian culture and of its destruction by the white invaders of the continent; and also that there is an irony in the fact that the many quotations from Jefferson, who fought for abolition, nevertheless reflect the most condescending assessment of the Negro's abilities. Citations from Franklin and Carnegie similarly urge a capitalist opportunism. Of course any such selection of themes will involve a radical mental rearrangement of the text by the reader who, aided by Butor's subtle typographical placing, thus partly cancels its discontinuities of form. It is this special challenge to co-operation and recreation which makes Butor's work a worthy successor to that of Carlos Williams.

II

Postmodern collage very frequently demands this kind of response, to a fictive environment which is to be perceived as discontinuous. As complex societies and their subcultures become ever more incomprehensible, more wilful in their incorporation of the merely contingent, so does art, which often aims at stark juxtaposition rather than family resemblance amongst its constituent parts. Perspective, to adapt Kenneth Burke, is more and more assumed to arise, like the genie from Aladdin's lamp, through mere incongruity, and should it sometimes fail to be perceived, a fall-back justification can always be given—'openness of form demands an openness of response'. This challenge, familiar to literary critics, has recently migrated to painting, and it cannot always be met. Most extreme in this respect, though in different ways, are Robert Rauschenberg and Jasper Johns, who in breaking away from abstract expressionism managed to stage a kind of Dada revival, which in many ways anticipated and then ran parallel to more accessible Pop-art styles.

Their collage work can be extremely perplexing. Modernist collage had usually inhabited a single and intelligible world. Since cubism, with its guitars, musical notation, wine glasses, and newsprint, there had been some attempt both to reflect a way of life, and to use the outlines of the elements of the collage to make an ingeniously satisfying formal design. Dada and surrealism had of course imported a frequently mysterious 'psychological' element, but had largely remained intelligible, particularly with respect to its stance within the society surrounding it. But Rauschenberg, looking back to Schwitters, and perhaps under the influence also of Olson and Cage, whom he encountered in his period at Black Mountain college from 1948 to 1949, produced documentary 'combine paintings' whose materials were much more disparate. His incorporation of collage elements can be as cavalier and as disconnected as the prose he uses to describe the process: 'The concept I plantation struggle to deal with ketchup is opposed to the logical continuity of lift tab inherent in laguage [*sic*] and communication. My fascination with images open 24 hrs is based on the complex interlocking of disparate visual facts heated pool that have no respect for grammar.'[32] Even if the prose and the paintings thus produced do reflect 'the sensory input of the city dweller and the industrial output of goods and waste'[33] it is doubtful whether they have any Waste Land-like common denominators, as any inventory of their contents will show. Thus in *Untitled* (1955) we have a postcard of a mansion house, a rosette, a picture of a naked girl sitting on a pile of logs, a printed card saying 'Does God Really Care?' smeared over with white paint, the head of a rooster, some children's writing and drawing under the heading 'Here is a picture I drew about playing away from traffic', a square piece of green material, and a piece of the marbling pattern used in book binding. And in *Small Rebus* (1956) we have magazine photos of sports events, a map section showing the North Central United States, a snapshot of a family, postage stamps, a child's drawing of a clock face, a horse's head, and a piece of flower-printed cloth, as well as the smudges of paint which flatten and bind the surface and are common to many of Rauschenberg's paintings of this type. It is very difficult to believe that these elements have anything binding them together in the way of thematic association; what they do have in common is their ready availability to the artist within a modern urban context. [See Pl. 8.]

Of course it is possible to make fairly convincing 'critical remarks' about Rauschenberg's materials taken separately: thus the marbling and the green material experiment with texture, the children's art contrasts as usual with the 'sophisticated' context in which it is being exploited, the news photos, and maps, and religious handouts are common icons for American society, and so on. But I am not convinced that this sort of talk can give us any real insight into the work as a whole. Treating these pictures as elementary scrapbooks for simple art lessons does not seem to be what is required. The relationships between these various images must thus remain largely private to their assembler, a Proustian array of evocative objects minus the narrative. It is not even clear to me that when we do have such associations revealed, they help much (thus the rooster in *Untitled* is supposed to refer to Rauschenberg's early pets, and is echoed in *Satellite* (1955) and *Odalisque* (1955–8)). There seems to be very little attempt at any very subtle formal pattern either, since many of the parts of these collages fall within a rectangular grid pattern, like those exploited some time ago by Max Ernst for more conventionally surrealist purposes in his paintings like *Vox Angelica* (1943). Such paintings thus point to a 'reading'—they are essentially literary, like a scrapbook,—and yet the key to their interpretation has not yet emerged, nor is it likely to. The most one can hope for, it seems, is a mild kind of surrealist shock, as for example in *Crocus* (1962) which incorporates images of a lorry, the *Rokeby Venus*, mosquitoes, a football, and a repetition of the cherub from the Velazquez. This painting is in no sense flower-like, though the juxtaposition of the traditional erotic aesthetic image with its uncouth companions, particularly the boring and ugly lorry, is disturbingly incongruous in a mild sort of way. [See Pl. 7.]

Such works are open to Wallace Stevens's accusation of traditional surrealism, that 'It invents without discovering', despite Rauschenberg's rather self-contradictory claim that he aims at 'an extremely complex random order that cannot be described as accidental'.[34] Invention, in the sense of finding, is easy on these terms, and it is difficult here to distinguish between the accidental, supposedly redeemed by the act of artistic making, and the merely slapdash. The wilful messiness of much of the brush work and around the images, in a kind of parody of abstract expressionism, does little to resolve the matter; if anything it makes Rauschenberg's work seem even more wilful and self-indulgent, its esotericism reflecting a fear of the 'obviousness' of any kind of intellectual discipline.

On the other hand, Rauschenberg's statements and work may be taken as symptomatic, of a deliberate rejection of the modernist myth of coherence behind fragmentation (the quest buried in *The Waste Land*, the private obsessions of Ernst). The result is an art which is deliberately disjunct, fractured, full of gaps which are supposed to do as much to reveal its meaning as its content does. In this it unwittingly comes close to the aesthetic of many structuralists like Pierre Macherey, who deconstruct works of art to reveal their inconsistencies, even whey they purport to be unified. The critic is thus encouraged to look for what the work fails to say (the 'non-dit' of the work) in the belief that such 'absences' reveal the inevitable self-contradictions of late-bourgeois society. The artist who cannot or will not 'get it all together' thus reveals in his abundant yet confused imagery the discordant complexities of the society in which he lives. But this kind of interpretation when applied to an artist like Rauschenberg, sociologically significant though it may be, does little to increase such satisfaction as may be derived from his paintings as works of art to be appreciated for themselves, rather than as symptoms of some general malaise.

Similar though rather less intractable difficulties assail us in many of the collage paintings by Jasper Johns, which (as those of Rauschenberg) incorporate motifs found frequently elsewhere in his own painting, but which do not seem to have established any very significant connotations, except of a strictly limited conceptualist kind. They merely refer us to other paintings. As Michael Crichton points out, or perhaps admits, 'Johns is an artist who has always been satisfied with a limited range of imagery, and who has said that his usual emotion when working is boredom.'[35] This gives Johns's work an undoubted unity, and shows him as a painter who has throughout his career worked hard to establish recognizable subjects—targets, flags, plaster casts, numbers, and so on, but who has failed or refused to give them any symbolic resonance when they are juxtaposed. Their small conceptualist points will never come together to make an argument. Thus one of his most monumental canvasses, the enigmatically entitled *According to What* (1974), contains a number of these past motifs: an inverted chair and the plaster cast of a leg, the title painted in packing-case lettering, model letters variously and contradictorily coloured and spelling RED YELLOW BLUE, with their 'shadows' painted on the canvas, a long strip of silk-screened news-print, yellow, red, and blue rectangles, and a bent wire coat-hanger. It is an anthology of motifs which can do little more than congratulate the beholder on his grasp of the artist's earlier work. [See Pl. 9.]

Part of the problem in interpreting this sort of painting lies in seeing how its elements relate to communication in society at large: it was the great merit of many pop painters, trivial as they were in other ways, that they were centrally concerned with this relationship, and it gives the painting of the best of them an impact far removed from the irritable hermeticism of Rauschenberg and Johns. They rely upon a hidden order which looks back to modernism and is essentially interpretable. Indeed many of them show a nostalgia for the modern period, in their tendency to pile up metaphorically related instances drawn from different levels in the culture. An example of this would be Peter Blake's *On the Balcony* (1955–7) which groups around four children sitting hieratically upon a park bench, many versions of people displayed on balconies, and allusions to this. Thus one child holds a version of Manet's famous picture, there are two *trompe-l'œil* photos of the Royal family outside Buckingham Palace, and another small girl stands on a table holding a copy of *Romeo and Juliet* (with its famous 'balcony scene'); and indeed further down the picture there is a pennant from Verona. The idea of lovers on a balcony is parodied by two doves standing outside a dovecote, and so on. A sort of 'common denominator rule' applies here, as the painting incorporates many metaphoric instances of its own procedures, which is that of a kind of hieratic self-display in public. Blake's technique of juxtaposition looks back even further in those of his works in which the elements actually are collaged, to the Victorian habit of pasting scraps on screens, as in his *Love Wall* of 1961. His nostalgia makes his appeal a rather touchingly conservative one, akin to that of John Betjeman in poetry. [See Pl. 10.]

Richard Hamilton, on the other hand, is much more typically of his own period, and indeed deliberately so. His

'Just what is it that makes today's homes so different, so appealing?'
which notoriously introduced the 'This is Tomorrow' exhibition in the Whitechapel Gallery in September 1956, deliberately worked through a shopping-list of contemporary
objects to be incorporated in the picture, largely by means of
magazine cuttings:

Man, woman. Food. History. Newspapers. Cinema. Domestic
appliances. Cars. Space. Comics. T.V. Telephone. Information.[36]

Two assistants clipped out possible images, and Hamilton
selected them according to their credible relative pro-
portions within a room interior. The ceiling is a photograph
of the earth from space, and the carpet on the floor is a
photograph of a crowd on a beach (a motif which occurs later
in Hamilton's work). The whole was meant to combine to
show different ways of transmitting information, admass
icons plundered from the communications industry: hence
the framed picture of the cover of *Young Romance* on the wall,
the tape-recorder on the floor, the cinema showing the *Jazz
Singer* outside, and all the other objects specified on the
original list, including the body-building man and the
pin-up who so incongruously inhabit the room.

This use of juxtaposed and externally derived popular
imagery continued to be a theme in Hamilton's work. As in
Duchamp, who is an influence, there is a gathering within
single works of discrete elements which are all brought into
satisfying relationship within the picture plane, however
disparate they may be in style and origin (photographic
illusionism, diagrams, abstract shapes, and so on). This is
most obvious in the *Interior* series, in which, much more
convincingly than in *'Just what is it . . .'*, which is chiefly
remarkable for its ingenuity, the elements combine in the
perspective of a room. Indeed the solution of a formal problem is always a consideration, as the inspection of Hamilton's studies for particular paintings and the variants of his
finished work will reveal. Thus *$he* (1958–61) depends on the
contrast between kitchen equipment, parts of the body, and
the dress of a model from *Esquire* magazine. In it, a
refrigerator, a toaster metamorphosed with a Hoover, and a

defrosting machine, are juxtaposed to a dress outline in shallow plywood relief (which functions also in the design as an apron), and a naked breast and neck. Two primary modes of communication in the popular media, the advertisement for consumer goods and the model photograph, are juxtaposed within the picture, in order to reveal a tension in the culture which surrounds it. Thus Hamilton says that

The worst thing that can happen to a girl, according to the ads, is that she should fail to be exquisitely at her ease in her appliance setting—the setting that now does much to establish our attitude to woman in the way that her clothes alone used to. . . .

The relationship of woman and appliance is a fundamental theme in our culture . . . Characteristic posture: inclination towards the appliance in a gesture of affectionate genuflection. Possessive but also bestowing. She offers the delights of the appliance along with her other considerable attributes.[37]

The advertisement typically affirms this relationship; there is an echo of this in Hamilton's painting, but it is also fragmented and subverted. The sentimental drama of possession is subordinated to an aesthetically satisfying series of formal relationships (the mere outline of the dress in relief, the cartoon-like metamorphosis of two appliances into one), which nevertheless retain some of the textural relationships seen by Hamilton as implicit in the original advertisement: 'the interplay of fleshy plastic, and smooth, fleshier metal'.[38] The basic design too, is inspired by a genuine appreciation of the techniques of the advertiser, and a sense of its possibilities for new types of perspective in serious art: 'The source of the overall layout of *$he* is a brilliant high shot of the cornucopic refrigerator—a view that uses a photographic convention from the auto ads. The Cadillac pink colour of this particular model of RCA Whirlpool's fridge/freezer was adopted with enthusiasm for the painting.'[39] [See Pl. 11.]

Much of the Pop painting of the same period as *$he*, by Boshier, Caulfield, Hockney, Allen Jones, and Kitaj (diverse as these actually are) also produced a play of signs of different kinds within the picture space, and thus relied upon models of communication of a sophisticated kind, as the picture plays with our recognition of its sources. Much collage of this type is a development out of Eliotic simultaneity, but without any of Eliot's conservative implications. For the elements within such pictures are not implicitly hierarchized as those within the modernist poem are, and indeed in many cases, like Blake's use of Manet (or even Rauschenberg's of Velazquez), or Hamilton's allusions to the Ingres odalisque image in *Pin Up*, there is a deliberate inversion of 'high' and 'low' elements, with the popular imagery dominant.

This stylistic transformation of the commonly available or public image, from photo-advertising, auto-styling, film, science fiction, comics, and so on, may have been camp or quaint or merely dated in some cases, but it always makes the viewer judge whether style has in fact redeemed content, as in Lichtenstein's use of the comic in *Whaam!* (1963), Peter Phillips's star photos, pin-ups and pinball machine styling in *For Men Only Starring B.B. and M.M.* (1961), Wesselman's combination of outline nudes and interior decoration, Robert Indiana's typographical arrangements, or even the echoes of glossy magazines in the supreme elegance of Hockney's swimming pools. In such cases a line has successfully been crossed between media-image and art. In others, it has not, as in Rosenquist's combination of car grill, face, and spaghetti in *I love you with my Ford* (1961), which hardly goes beyond the bill poster, or Mel Ramos's posing of pin-up girls with animals, as in *Gorilla* (1967), or (in another inversion of the values implicit in earlier painting on mythological themes) in *Leta and the Pelican* (1969), which is as conventionally sexy as *Playboy*. (And, one might add, as engagingly artificial—for surely the gatefold marks the final confusion between flesh and plastic, the human being and the doll.)

III

Collage technique in music has a relatively long modernist history, from Charles Ives's Symphony No. 4 to Shostakovitch's Symphony No. 15 (and the Beatles' *Sergeant Pepper*, whose prodigality and nostalgia is closely analogous to that of 'Pop' painting). Such works express a similar relationship to that noticed before between high and low in visual art, as the 'new' work incorporates allusions to more familiar and popular music. The method is an essentially literary one; for just as the painting plays with and attempts to reconcile the contradictory codes of communication from which its signs are derived, so the musical work supplements its own symphonic argument (or song in the Beatles' case) with echoes and allusions whose relationship to their parent work seems to be an essentially ironic one: as in Shostakovitch's sly allusions to Rossini and Wagner. One is led to suspect a hidden programme, a drama beyond the music. A particularly interesting postmodern example of this is the third movement of Luciano Berio's *Sinfonia* (1968) for it further illustrates our principle of the foreground assemblage of apparently unrelated materials, contrasted to a background of order (as in *Stimmung*). In this piece, the fragmentary quotation is literally carried along by the rhythmic impulse of the third movement of Mahler's Second Symphony. As Berio says, 'The Mahler movement is treated like a container within whose framework a large number of references are proliferated, interrelated and integrated into the flowing structure of the original work itself.' Mahler's triple ländler-rhythm thus carries fragments of Bach, Schoenberg, Debussy, Ravel, Strauss, Berlioz, Brahms, and so on (up to Boulez and Stockhausen); and buried within all these musical events is a performance by the Swingle singers of a text from Beckett's *The Unnameable*, bits of Joyce, slogans from the May 'événements', and so on. Berio claims that the relationship between words and music here is one of 'interpretation, almost as Traumdeutung, of that stream-of-consciousness-like flowing, which is the most expressive character of Mahler's movement'.[40] If this is a stream of consciousness, then its hidden drama is a very personal one: and in fact the relationship between Beckett, 'recorded dialogues with my friends and family', and quotation from works like *La Mer* or *La Valse* chiefly owes its effectiveness to the skill with which Berio has made all these separate parts recognizable and to the hypnotic drive given to the whole by the rhythms of Mahler's ländler. For as in some of the painting we have discussed, there is not much metaphorical bridgework here. As Berio admits, the work is 'not so much composed as it is assembled, to make possible the mutual transformation of the component parts'. Although the latter is a much more arbitrary process, it is justified here, if by anything, by the fact that it is the listener's own perception of the dramatic contrast between the parts (for example the anguished muttering of the singers counterposed to serene quotations from Ravel) that brings about this 'mutual transformation' as one kind of experience qualifies another.

Much more genuinely a stream of consciousness, and using a very similar technique, is Berio's *Recital I (for Cathy)* (1972). This work exploits the full range of the singer's expression, under the burden of her own (and by implication history's) repertoire, so that the piece is not only a psychological study, but projects the way in which our artistic inheritance may bear upon all of us. 'These fragments I have shored against my ruins.' The dramatic development of the piece chiefly depends upon a stream-of-consciousness text provided by Berio, very much in the style of Beckett. This is interwoven with fragments from Cathy Berberian's known repertory: we thus have snatches of Ravel, Milhaud, Hahn, Falla, Bach, and Schubert, as well as operatic excerpts from *Carmen*, *Manon*, *Lakmé*, and so on. The choice between these is largely left to the singer, and is governed by the tonality (or atonality) required. The result is an unbearable psychological tension, a kind of florid version of Beckett's late monologues, particularly *Not I*; indeed a similarly schizophrenic effect is achieved. This is reinforced by the fact that there are three different types of accompaniment in the piece; a solo piano, two other pianos (one on the platform and the other in the orchestra), and a chamber orchestra, so that the instrumental texture is divided up in a way that reflects the warring aspects of the recitalist's personality.

At the beginning, the singer is without her accompanist (who arrives only half-way through), and so has to rely upon the chamber orchestra. She begins with Monteverdi's 'La

lettera amorosa'. Matters become more and more complicated, to the point at which the singer is trying not only to
perform parts of her repertoire, but also to give a lecture on
music theatre: 'the only form where gesture sound and
meaning coincide is the ritual.' But she suddenly breaks off:
'Now lets see now here we have five men with masks and
instruments naturally', and from this point on she herself is
involved in a disturbing ritual of the kind she has specified.
For five masked men from the orchestra now invade the
stage, wearing *commedia dell'arte* masks. The climax inevitably approaches, for all the time she has been performing, a
wardrobe mistress has been adding to the recitalist's cos-
tume, and at the end, she is also enmeshed in a net. The last
part of Berio's text is a cry of anguish at her bizarre situation,
in which we have perceived her symbolic imaginings and
fears in literal enactment:

> this lesson continues and we speak and no dreams of what we really
> think we worry about keeping on that ragged mask of intelligence
> sensitivity mercy and conscience this absence of explosions is
> unbearable even without those instruments which play and play
> and play until they drive me mad and devour me what are you
> looking at? why don't you do something? laugh laugh! do some-
> thing anything don't be afraid! applaud! applaud! . . . 'libera nos'

The music of the piece ends correspondingly, with a coda-
like *lied* in which the vocal line is itself trapped between the
notes C and C sharp, around which it obsessively revolves.
The work as a whole finally breaks through to a continuous
lyricism; but it is a song of despair.

   This piece is a most impressive development of a tradition
which descends from *Erwartung*. Berio has always been fascinated by the musical and psychological problems raised by
the solo female voice, and has developed them further in
other directions in two pieces whose techniques are very
different: *Sequenza III* for solo voice, and *Visage* (1961) for
magnetic tape, based on the voice of Cathy Berberian and
electronic sounds. But these do not employ that collage
technique of citation we have just analysed, which produces
psychologically enclosed dramatic works with room for the

surprising, but not for the radically contingent; and they stay, rather, within the terms of pure music, the literary text, and their mutually interlocking history.

The more extreme collagists in music have however invented similarly psychologically embracing works which also include non-musical sounds, and thus attempt to forge a connection between 'music' and 'the world'. Stockhausen's *Hymnen* (1966–7) is at the moment one of the most ambitious experiments with collage of this type. It uses a mixture of electronic sounds, conventional music (the national anthems upon which the work is based), and concrete sounds, all variously distorted at times, in a kind of palimpsest of all possible audible experiences, from swamp ducks through the calls of a croupier and crowd sounds, to the composer's own breathing and his recital of the names of all the women he has loved.

We can I think get an idea of the methods involved here by concentrating upon a single section for which we have Stockhausen's own account. He describes the close of the fourth 'region' of the work (which is dedicated to Berio) in revealingly pictorial terms:

First I made a picture without a frame—you hear a section of the anthem of Ghana with people dancing to very fast drum rhythms and one man's voice calling out 'Ho-ah-ho-ho'. Next, after some breathing, make a stroke for the left side of the frame. This stroke is like a vertical line comprising many pitches, a cluster with a chord,—very loud. And then you hear the Russian anthem chopped up with an electronic chopper.

These snatches of the *Internationale* are distorted as if passing through an unstable electronic circuit. Unfortunately much of *Hymnen* deliberately offers the frustrations of a badly tuned wireless set. The work begins with a barrage of short-wave static, and however much this may be taken to symbolize the difficulties of international communication and the 'given' nature of much of Stockhausen's material, plucked out of the air so to speak, it blurs, no doubt deliberately, the contrast for the listener between the electronic modification of sound and the purely accidental distortion of bad tuning.

Each stage of the framing processes which follow in this final section repeats a version of the 'stroke' on the left-hand side (speaker): thus in the third stage, the *Internationale* combines with the sound of applauding crowds and of horses 'and especially the clacking of the wheels of coaches as they go over cobblestones—I took these sounds from a recording of a reception given to the English Queen in an African town.' In the fourth stage, the British anthem is combined with further crowd noises, culminating (appropriately enough, one may feel) with a soccer match cheer; and in the fourth, we have the Indian anthem and melodic passages on the shenai. The final sequences of the work are dominated by Stockhausen's own breathing and his voice 'saying "pluramon" very slowly—it's like an artist who signs his own painting'. The following section juxtaposes sounds recorded in a shop in China and those of a student protest at the technical High School in Aachen—fashionable ones for the time of composition. Then

Just before the last stage you hear me saying once more 'Pluramon'—this time quickly—followed by the first stroke (the pitches between the top and the bottom now make a perfect fifth six octaves apart). And in the form of this seventh insert, we finally find the empty frame which lasts ninety seconds. There's the breathing inside and this high and low sound. The low sound is really like a lion roaring, incredibly low and strong with all the harmonies inside trembling, very rich in timbre, and penetrating right into the stomach. Then comes the final stroke, closing the frame, and at the top of it, a loud shrieking bird cry, disappearing quickly in an echo space. We hear a few more breathings—very slow—and finally one last breath, a short inhalation and accentuated exhalation shorter than the previous ones. Out, and that's the end. [41]

It is noteworthy that Stockhausen describes the elements of the work as 'sound pictures'; and Jonathan Cott, to whom in an interview, he made the remarks quoted, points out truly that many listeners will not notice the technical transformations that Stockhausen works electronically upon his sources, and simply approach the work as 'some kind of pop art collage'. This seems very just, despite the fact that Stockhausen insists that he has in fact produced an alchemical metamorphosis of natural sounds: 'I'm interested in revealing how, at a special moment, a human sound is that of a duck and a duck's sound is the silver sound of shaking metal fragments.'[42]

The effect is to a large degree like that of a radio programme, in which we have a number of detailed and yet distorted sound effects, but no dialogue, no drama, no narrative. Stockhausen's attempt at a contrasting universalization of his work by taking national anthems as the base for his electronically transformed musical quotations is only partly successful, since they do not exactly raise an echo in every heart in their original forms, and the conventions for their electronic transformation are often in any case no clearer to the listener than the other harmonic procedures adopted by Stockhausen which we have discussed earlier. The section I have discussed is nevertheless one of the most impressive in the work, and reveals its essentially meditative nature, as the plethora of sounds in the work finally narrows down to the private world of their artistic creator. *Hymnen* is thus akin in its way to *Stimmung* and *Carré*, and also, in its prodigality of invention, to Rauschenberg. If, however, we try to discern a developing stream of consciousness in it, we find that it is one which is peculiarly private. Even though the four regions of the work do reveal quite distinct sound worlds, they lack a clear articulation, and one is frequently forced into a passive admiration of its different effects, which are indeed striking, in a rather Cineramic way, when the work is performed as it should be, in a large hall with a full range of speakers, so that its spatial movements are dramatically perceptible. It is a highbrow version of the Pink Floyd.

Stockhausen has always treated music as a transformational art, despite the fragmentary effect if often has, even upon the technically adept listener. John Cage (to whom the third region of *Hymnen* is dedicated) makes assumptions about music which are far more extreme than this. His *Variations IV* for example, although it is as eclectic as Stockhausen's work, makes no attempt to transform its sound sources in the service of a design. The work is a wholly arbitrary mixture of street noises, sounds in the gallery in which the work is performed (in the recording), taped bits of radio broadcasts, interviews, language records, bits of pop, jazz, laughing records, church bells, medical lectures, and so on. Within this mêlée of words, music, and concrete sounds, are quoted a huge range of popular and not so popular classical musical works, including *Carnaval*, the *Symphonie Fantastique*, Mozart's G Minor Symphony, Beethoven's Third, Fifth, Sixth, and Ninth Symphonies, the 'Hallelujah' chorus, the 'Anvil' chorus, *Bolero*, Bach's D minor Toccata, and many others. As Saltzman succinctly puts it, 'This is . . . the kitchen sink sonata, the everything piece, the minestrone masterpiece of modern music, the universe symphony of everybody and everything.'[43] Each element of this piece means no more than itself and is 'controlled' by nothing more than the original artistic context. As for much of the conceptual art we looked at earlier, and the 'happening', to which so much of Cage's work is akin, it is the simple fact of performance by an 'artist' that secures aesthetic attention. Yet the notion of expressivity hardly applies, for as soon as we catch on to the significance of one fragment it is immediately contradicted or obliterated by another. In this and other works Cage indeed achieves one of his main aims, which is to 'give up the desire to control sound, clear his mind of traditional music, and set about discovering means to let sounds be themselves rather than vehicles for man-made theories or the expression of human sentiments'.[44]

Both Stockhausen's and Cage's works are 'metacollage' very much in the sense that Stockhausen defines it, as 'going beyond the collage', in that 'pluralistic spirit that appeared after the last war; the so-called global village and tourism helped purvey this spirit . . . Collage is gluing together and seeing what happens. It's not really mediation. And collage is exactly what's happening in society. New York is a social collage.'[45] The reference here to McLuhan is typical: quite apart from the extraordinary social assumptions behind this sort of thinking, there lies also an acceptance of McLuhanesque theses concerning the way in which experience in the 'Electric Age' will cease to present itself to us serially, in the bad old Gutenberg manner, will give up linear patterns of causal sequence, and will increasingly appear to us in fields of simultaneous interaction. This is indeed very like the effect of *Hymnen* and *Variations IV* as works of art. But whether this actually reflects the reality around us is another matter. For although *Hymnen* is indeed set in a context of short-wave broadcasts and radio programmes, it is far from clear that these actually bind together human society in the way McLuhan specifies: indeed one may feel that such a view can only be made plausible by an effect of art, as in Stockhausen and Cage, and McLuhan's own rhetoric. Works like these are in fact deliberately trying to break down that mechanism which psychologists call selective attention, and for ends which are to say the least obscure. Cage's work in particular seems to me to present an artful disorder far beyond anything we could tolerate in 'real life' for more than a few hours.

Chapter Three: III. Chance

The art which repudiates rational control by allowing chance or indeterminacy into the creative or performing process always seems innovatory, for the rather special reason among others, that its very arbitrariness and lack of convention make it seem original. By definition, it excludes elements which repeat themselves from one work to another. It is permanently surprising, often unintelligible, and thus unsettling and shocking, typical indeed of 'avant-garde activity' as popularly conceived. We have thus reached the opposite pole from that theory-dominated, obsessively over-determined art which we discussed in our second chapter.

One of the easiest ways to achieve such a chance configuration is simply to throw the elements of the work on the floor, like dice; as in Carl André's *Spill (scatter piece)* (1966). Another method is to perpetuate in art apparently insignificant, purely contingent, and unplanned states of affairs. Thus one might collect together formless piles of rubbish, as in Fernandez Arman's *Poubelle (dustbin) I* (1960). Much of the work of Daniel Spoerri has a similar rationale: he glues or nails to any available surface whatever he happens to find on his table or in his studio—plates, left-over food, painting utensils, dirty ashtrays—anything that is around. In this way 'situations discovered by chance in order or disorder are fixed (trapped) just as they are upon their support of the moment (chair, table, box etc), only the orientation with respect to the spectator is altered. The result is declared to be a work of art (attention—work of art).'[46] Thus his *Tableau Piège* (1966) 'traps' a chamber-pot, the head of a madonna, an umbrella, a bicycle wheel, three shirts, a pair of shoes, a painting, and a pair of trousers, amongst other objects.

It is difficult however to use chance techniques convincingly in the visual and plastic arts, since whatever the method of production, the *result* looks intended, or at least selected, by the artist. The effect of Spoerri's work is thus as artful as the Rauschenbergian assemblage which it so much resembles. The chance method by which it evolves is simply not discernible within the work. It is thus the sequential arts of literature and music in which such methods can really dominate, since our experience of the work can be made to seem just as subject to the unpredictable event as the method of composition was.

William Burroughs makes the matter seem very simple: 'take a page more or less of your own writing, or from any writer living or dead. Cut into sections with scissors or switchblade as preferred and rearrange the sections. Looking away. Now write out the result . . .'[47] This method is in fact intended to make it possible for writers to use the collage methods of painting, and an early result was *The Exterminators* (1960), which Burroughs wrote in collaboration with Brion Gysin. It was perhaps a logical development from the earlier *Naked Lunch* (1959), a work without any real narrative continuity or constancy in its point of view. Its episodes simply co-exist, and the effect is one of reading the strip cartoons of trash magazines in a disordered and incomplete sequence. (This is small compensation for being encouraged by Burroughs to start in at any point we please.)

The didactic and admonitory *Nova Express* (1964) follows on from these. It is like a film wholly at the mercy of its own montage: 'Take orgasm noises stir and cut them in with torture and accident groans and screams sir and operating room jokes sir and flicker sex and torture films right with it sir.'[48] It is obscene and tedious, and so dulls the mind and prevents it from making connections anyway. To look for continuity may be wrong: to find it is worse, because when discerned it reveals an order which the aesthetic of the work seeks to deny. Nevertheless, the book is basically a science fiction fantasy, whose premiss is that earth has been invaded by extra-territorial gangsters—the Nova Mob—who infiltrate earthly institutions and encourage evil. They are pursued by the Nova Police, with their 'antibiotic handcuffs'.[49] The mythology is one of war within a drug-ridden 'inner space', in which 'word begets image and image is virus'.[50] Indeed one of the basic fantasies of the book is of a complete viral–technological programming of man, 'his brain seared by flash blasts of image war',[51] and a number of such key images, of nova ovens, orgasm death, image banks, oven ambushes, monster crabs, co-ordinate points, words falling, and spinal fluid (as in the typical sentence 'Two Lesbian agents with glazed faces of grafted penis flesh sat sipping spinal fluid through alabaster straws'),[52] flow through the book. Throughout, the two modes of conditioning, 'virus power' as symbolizing the oppression of society, and drug addiction, are in counterpoint, the one being made a confused metaphor for the other. Thus the book supposedly attacks 'all the boards syndicates and governments of the earth' but can only see them in terms of perversion and drug addiction, as making 'filth deals consummated in what lavatory to take what is not yours'.[53]

Burroughs asserts that 'In my writing I am acting as a map maker, an explorer of psychic areas . . . a cosmonaut of inner space.'[54] But whether this allows us to see his books as special pathological types of the stream of consciousness is a moot point. They are certainly dreamlike and hallucinatory, intermittently shot through with vivid fragments. Reality, inside or outside the body, is seen as terrifying, and the effect is nightmarish. But the cut-up technique surely makes inaccessible much of the subconscious motivation and unspoken linkage that we can look for in most connected stream-of-consciousness or even surrealist work, and which would give it a coherent stance. Thus a typical paragraph runs:

Smell of cigarette smoke on child track—Proceed to the outer—All marble streets and copper domes inside air—Signature in scar tissue stale and rotten as the green water—Moldy pawn ticket by purple fungoid gills the invisible siamese twin moving in through flesh grafts and visual patterns—exchanging weight—on slow purple gills—Addicts of the purpose—Flesh juice vampires is no good—All sewage—Idiot smiles eating erogenous deal—Sweet rotten smell of ice—Insect smell of the green car wreck—The young agent to borrow your body for a special half made no face to conceal the ice—He dies many years ago—He said: 'Yes you want to—Right back to a size like that—Said on child track—Screaming on the deal?'[55]

Indeed technique and psychological interest are inevitably in conflict here, as that Gutenberg linearity of print which parallels the Jamesian stream is attacked, in an attempt to 'rub out the word'. In the process, language is used to destroy itself. However much a spontaneous factor may be desired, so that the mind can be released from the oppressive controls of society (shades of Robbe-Grillet here, as elsewhere), the paranoiac inner myth suggests precisely the opposite. Our author is trapped in the mess he has made. There is thus a basic conflict both within and beyond Burroughs's work, which cripples any gestures it may make towards any larger ideological significance.

So far as music is concerned, chance operations and performer choice were originally seen in Europe as offering a path divergent from the strict controls of the serialist mode, and the result was Stockhausen's *Klavierstück XI*, of 1956. (However, it must be pointed out, both that John Cage in America had long before been a devoted exponent of chance methods, without any need for post-war serialism as a stimulus; and that Boulez had hit upon a similar method in the 'Constellation-miroir' section of his Third Piano Sonata, which was begun before Stockhausen's work, but performed after it.) In all these cases, one may feel that there was a strong influence from the visual arts—music becomes in some instances a kind of audible mobile, of fixed elements but no constant outline. This is, I think, particularly true of *Klavierstück XI*, in which we have 'controlled chance'. The composer's directions for the piece are as follows:

On a single sheet of paper (59 by 93cm) 19 different note groups are irregularly distributed. The following directions for performance appear on the reverse side of the sheet:
The player casts a random glance at the sheet of paper and begins with whichever group he sees first; this he plays . . . at any speed he chooses, at any basic dynamic level, and using any mode of attack. Once the first group has come to an end, he reads the ensuing indications of speed ($T°$), basic dynamic level and mode of attack, casts a further random glance to find another of the groups, and plays this in accordance with the three indications he has found.

The work ends when a group is reached for the third time. Stockhausen displays a typical confidence in the permanent validity of his latest experimental methods, in asserting that writing music 'after this' involves 'making a direct approach to the musician's living organism'[56] so that performances can be both multiple and unpredictable. Performer choice, whether 'organic', or more likely, derived from practice in performing the piece effectively as in jazz, is indeed the crucial element here, as it is in many other works by Stockhausen, Boulez, and Berio, but it nearly always takes place within a context in which certain ground rules are clearly specified (as we saw in the case of *Stimmung*).

In much of John Cage's music, however, nothing of the kind applies. Compromises with the generic expectations we have learnt from past tradition, control of content, and even questions of value, are pushed to one side. We are entirely at the mercy of the artist and the process of performance he invents, and have to accept what happens without question, certainly without any attempt to make ordered sense of it, as Cage's own remarks on composition in his book *Silence* make clear:

> It is . . . possible to make a musical composition the continuity of which is free of individual taste and memory (psychology) and also of the literature and 'traditions' of the art. The sounds enter the time space centred within themselves, unimpeded by service to any abstraction, their 360 degrees of circumference free for an infinite play of interpenetration. Value judgments are not in the nature of this work as regards either composition, performance, or listening. The idea of relation (the idea:2) being absent, anything (the idea:1) may happen. A 'mistake' is beside the point, for once anything happens it authentically is.[57]

A revealing example of these principles in operation, mistakes included, may be found in Cage's *Imaginary Landscapes* for twelve radios, with two players at each, one for tuning and the other for dynamics, Cage conducting. The tempo, dynamics, and structure for this work were chance-derived from the *I Ching* method of tossing coins, and the actual sounds we hear depend entirely on what happens to be on the wavebands to which the wirelesses are tuned at the time of performance. The first performance of this work took place too late in the evening for there to be much there at all, and was not much of a success in consequence. Cage's attitude about this 'was one of comparative indifference, since he believes the concept to be more interesting than the result of any single performance'.[58]

Stoicism is indeed perhaps the key response to the performance and hearing of such works. One is privileged to be in the presence of an 'artist' working out his 'idea' (1 or 2, it hardly matters). This seems to me to be neatly symbolized in Cage and Hiller's *HPSCHD* (1967–9) in which a brave little harpsichord seems to be trying to play Mozart against a storm of interference, like a bird singing in the middle of a blitz. The music for *HPSCHD* was simply part of a huge environmental set-up in the Assembly Hall at the University of Illinois. Fifty-two projectors showed films and slides, mirrored balls reflected dots of light in all directions, and the sounds came from fifty-eight amplified channels, fifty-one of these simultaneously broadcasting computer-generated music controlled by four independently operated tape-recorders. As all these sounds were also produced by Cage's randomizing *I Ching* procedures, the result was, as Richard Kostelanetz has noted, 'a supremely microtonal chaos'. He continues:

On top of this mix, one could hear seven amplified harpsichords, for HPSCHD is that word reduced to the characters necessary for computer transmission. Three were playing fixed versions of Mozart's late eighteenth century 'Introduction to the Composition of Waltzes by means of Dice' in which the performer is allowed to play sections in any order he chooses. With computer assistance, Cage and Hiller realised three different fixed versions of the fragments, two of which incorporate other passages from Mozart. Two more harpsichordists . . . played through differing but individually fixed collages of harpsichord music from Mozart to the present, while David Tudor played 'computer print out for twelve tone gamut'. The seventh keyboard operator . . . had nothing more specific than blanket permission to play any Mozart he wished; and every instrumentalist received the further instruction: 'In addition to playing his own solo, each harpsichordist is free to play any of the others'.[59]

The commercial recording of *HPSCHD* compromises a little: it uses only three of the harpsichord parts, but compensates to some degree for this slight reduction of chaos by containing a computer-printed set of randomized instructions which allows the individual listener to use the volume and tone controls on each channel of his gramophone to produce further variations upon the piece. It is in fact difficult to hear the difference between one such playing and another—since this is chance music, and we cannot by definition make sense of chance events *per se*, the result is just as chaotic. The fact that we are 'controlling' it in some way makes little difference to the result. Thus Cage and other artists discussed in this section often waste good ideas by losing them in a mess.

Indeterminacy and chance have been very fashionable in the postmodern period: they are to some degree guarantors of that irrationalism and repudiation of control which artists previously had to simulate by some kind of supposedly random psychic automatism (now metamorphosed into 'performer choice'). The exploitation of chance, in cases like that of *HPSCHD*, also has a satisfying primitivism (the casting of dice) allied to an overbearing exploitation of computer technology. This finds its echo in the simplicities of the cut-up technique (you only need a pair of scissors) when it is used by Burroughs in the service of a myth of technological bombardment, by alien or at least alienating powers.

Of course in every case the basic elements of the work have been chosen by the artist, in gross if not in detail, but he need have no notion of the ultimate effect of his work on an audience. Indeed the success of the indeterminate work must very largely depend upon the goodwill of that sort of person who is capable of picking up 'good vibes' from almost anything. Much of the collaged and indeterminate art we have discussed has to rely upon us for its real creation. Since we cannot in fact tolerate chaos for long, we have to impose on it short-term pockets of order and intelligibility. For some this may ensure a satisfying privacy of response as the work is literally what we make of it; others may feel that they are simply being tortured by the arbitrary.

PART THREE: POLEMIC

Chapter Four: The Avant-Garde and the Culture

The notion of the avant-garde has given a great deal of trouble. It was a political term in origin, and so in a sense it remains. Any historical consideration of it thus leads to all sorts of problems concerning the nature of avant-garde groupings (which in our period run from the abstract expressionists in New York in the 1940s to Boulez's IRCAM in Paris in the 1970s), the methods by which they propagate their ideas, their relationship to the state of society, and so on. But these are sociological questions which I do not wish to pursue, since I have not attempted to give a comprehensive or chronological account of experimental art, and have preferred to concentrate upon a limited number of essentially technical and aesthetic changes by which major contemporary artists freed themselves from the assumptions of modernism.

Many of them nevertheless fulfilled the very traditional modernist role of cultural agitator. We can thus see Boulez as the (parricidal) heir to Schoenberg, Cage and Rauschenberg as continuing to astound audiences in the manner of Breton and Duchamp, and so on. Many of the major artists of the postmodern period have in fact been remarkable for their messianic energies, particularly amongst the musicians, where competition, focused in the early 1950s upon the contemporary music festivals at Darmstadt and Donaueschingen, was peculiarly direct. Indeed Messiaen, Boulez, Stockhausen, and Cage are remarkable not only for their music but also for the number of words they have written to explain and defend it, from the technical austerities of Boulez's *Penser la musique aujourd'hui*, to the Dada lecture-performances of Cage. The major new novelists also (with the notable exception of Claude Simon) seem to have divided their labour in a similar fashion. This combination of creation and polemic is perhaps to be expected in an age in which, as I have argued, critical concerns not only motivate artists, but are integral to their works.

The boundaries between criticism and creation are as blurred as can be in the dandy-aesthete tradition of Wilde and Cocteau, which has been sustained in the contemporary period by John Cage and Andy Warhol in particular—two artists whose own mode of existence has claimed significance along with their art. For these two, artistic performances, surprisingly or bathetically dominated by chance, or by deliberately trivial imagery (money, soup cans, Brillo boxes, flowers, cows' heads) function above all as a sign of the artist at work. The great problem for them is thus as much what to *do* next as what to make next, since the product, however parasitic it may be upon theory, only seems authentic in the light of the personality and beliefs of the artist, of Cage's Zen Buddhism or Warhol's absurdist high camp. How it comes out (from randomly tuned wireless sets, or by putting notes where there are imperfections in the music paper,[1] or with the paint actually applied by assistants from 'The Factory') is of less importance than the fact that the process is presided over by an artist whose verbal articulacy fills in the gaps between one work of art and another. For even if the work can be left to chance or to inspiration (let's make a film an hour long of *Taylor Mead's Ass* (1964)) the personality of the artist cannot. As Cage's many writings and lectures, themselves works of art, and Warhol's brilliantly funny autobiography both testify, the real wit and invention and the really constant effort go into the artist's personality and thoughts. Not for them the quasi-scientific claims to objective research of Boulez or Butor or LeWitt. Like all true aesthetes they attempt to break down the barriers between art and life (their own). The actual production of works of art is the by-product of an attitude which dissolves all questions of value. One could apply to Cage and Warhol Camus's remark that 'The absurd creator does not prize his work. He could repudiate it',[2] if they had not already done so in effect themselves: hence the epigraph to Cage's *Silence*, 'Nothing is accomplished by writing/-hearing/-playing a piece of music. Our ears are now in excellent condition', or Warhol's saying that 'I think somebody should be able to do all my paintings for me . . . I think it would be so great if more people took up silk screens so that no-one would know whether a picture was mine or someone else's.'[3]

Such activities are salutary, whatever one may think of the result, because they remind us that what emerges from the often grouped activites of the avant-garde is the individual artist's sensibility; that although experimental music or the new novel or a new style in abstract painting may dictate alliances for the purposes of early promotion, what we are going to be left with in the end, if past history is anything to go by, is a unique work of art attributable to a particular artist. One is forcibly reminded of this basic truth, when considering the work of Beckett. He is surely one of the master figures of our age, and yet he doesn't much assert himself. 'Cultural agitator' is perhaps too vigorous a term to apply to him. He works in isolation, and he doesn't issue any manifestos. Yet it would be hard to deny his dominance, or the remarkable fact that he has managed to bring nearly every avant-garde technical advance within the compass of his own writing and beliefs, to be both an influence and a distiller of essences. Hence the combinatorial logic of *Watt* and its successors, which we find throughout the new novel; the relationship to popular art of *Godot* and the bleak comedy of *End Game*; the musical organization of *Play*; the minimalist 'happening/environment' with voice-over of *Breath*; the rigorously repetitive fragmentation of *Comment c'est*; and the appalled monologue of *Not I*, in which the mouth perceived through a curtain is reminiscent at one and the same time of the paintings of Francis Bacon and the anguished fragmentation and schizophrenia of Berio's *Recital-1*. He has even used chance methods in *Lessness*, a prose poem for which he shuffled sixty sentences originally written in six thematically related groups.[4] These sixty sentences were withdrawn one by one from a container and twice rearranged into twelve paragraphs, whose number of sentences from 3 to 7 was predetermined by a numerical scheme. Beckett's originality here and elsewhere is of course not what is in question; what emerges is his ability to take avant-garde techniques and subject them to the expression of his own unique vision with an economy and point that all too often escapes his contemporaries. Unlike many of them he has something of importance to say and need not disguise the lack of this behind the smoke-screen of technique.

The didactic energy, public display, and moral authority

of the various leaders of the avant-garde has, since the early 1960s at least, had its effect. In most areas of artistic activity but particularly in music and painting it is in control. This is not simply in the tautologous sense in which the experimentalist is in control of the 'progress of art', whatever that may be, but also in a more practical sense as well, particularly in the visual arts, which have always made the clearest distinction between progressives and conservative reactionaries (who produce portraits of horses and of persons of social consequence). Indeed Clement Greenberg, who did much to define the critical context in which painting since abstract expressionism has been seen, goes so far as to assert that 'since the fifties confessedly academic art has fallen out of sight. Today the only conspicious fine art—the exceptions, however numerous, are irrevelant—is avant-garde or what looks like or refers to avant-garde art.'[5]

One is inclined to agree with this, not because contemporary art has swept everyone up in a single line of progress (though abstract expressionism, serialism, and the new novel did attempt this in the 1950s) but for the opposite reason, that the avant-garde is all devouring because it has the virtue of being stylistically pluralist and historically aware, even if it is also obsessed by novelty and change. Indeed, a rather jokey sensibility now allows for a camp incorporation of the past, provided it is suitably distanced by technique. Thus one of the most recent movements in painting, Superrealism (or New Realism, or Photorealism, or Hyperrealism—the confusion of terminology is symptomatic of the different ways in which artists catch on to the latest -ism) can even turn back to incorporate that very academic realist art which Greenberg thought had fallen out of sight. Thus many of the paintings of horses by Richard McLean are Stubbs updated to the brasher social context of America, by implication doing what the old masters would have done if only they had had the benefit of modern photographic techniques.

This type of movement maintains the dynamic of the avant-garde in two ways. It reacts against what went before (in this case the dead ends of conceptualism and minimalism), and justifies itself not so much by content as by technique. Thus it uses the photograph in reproducing say, a postcard on a huge scale, or emphasizes an all-over sharp focus, a clarity of perception which the eye, even of the camera, never achieves, as in the portraits of Chuck Close and much of the work of Goings and Estes.

The causes of this eclecticism are interesting and I think of crucial importance for the vitality and accessibility of much postmodern art. As we saw in Chapter 2, its beginnings in the 1950s were theory-dominated, stylistically extremely purist and often austere. (Thus Boulez once wrote an article entitled 'Against hedonism in music'.) I believe that the catalyst for a huge expansion of stylistic range and psychological appeal, in all the arts came in the late 1950s and early 1960s with Pop art. This as an organized movement soon came to an end, leaving behind a number of artists like Lichtenstein and Rosenquist, whose work was closely tied to its assumptions. But its longer term effects were far more important than the monumental reproduction of comic strips or billboards in oil on canvas. For one thing, if its premisses concerning the interaction of different levels of culture could be accepted, it could offer a much needed reconciliation between advanced technical means, pleasure, and intelligibility. At the outset it did indeed provoke a conflict amongst critics, between those who like Clement Greenberg were committed to the rigours of abstract expressionism and therefore looked down upon the mass media as providing an 'ersatz culture . . . destined for those who are insensible to the value of genuine culture'[6] and those who believed with Lawrence Alloway that 'the new role of the fine arts is to be one of the possible forms of communication in a framework that also includes the mass arts'.[7] I believe that Alloway was largely right and that art progressed on the lines he suggests. This was partly in reaction against the very private feeling which lay behind the abstract designs of Newman, Kline, Guston, Rothko, and Still in America, or artists like Pasmore in Britain, in favour of the more public expression of feeling in a figurative style. Hence the production of a number of rather equivocal parodies of immediately previous art, as in Jim Dine's *Striped Saw Horse Piece* (1968–9), or Lichenstein's huge enlargements of abstract expressionist brushstrokes (Kline in the mode of Hokusai) in *Yellow and Green Brushstrokes* (1966), or *Big Painting No 6* (1965). But the effect of 'Pop' was not simply to reintroduce mimetic commitment to art. It also produced a reorientation of the attitudes of many experimental artists to the society they lived in. The distance between art and life, or at least the urban environment and its modes of communication, was radically foreshortened. Thus as Rosenberg asserts, since 'Pop': 'No influential American art movement has been either overtly or passively hostile to the majority culture. On the contrary, the leading idea in Pop, Op, colour field minimal and kinetic art, and in Happenings, has been to exorcise the negative impulses that tormented the earlier vanguard.'[8] One result of this has been to make the art museums of the 1970s much more relaxed places to be in. The visitor should be reassured that not all the work displayed aspires to the level of 'high art', that the joke (Oldenburg's *Soft Washstand* (1965) or *Soft Giant Drum Set* (1967) or Warhol's Brillo boxes), may be found alongside the demanding (as in Rothko), and the surrealistically disturbing (from Rauschenberg to Kienholz and Segal).

There was thus a relaxation and eclecticism of attitudes which reflected a change in the balance of the culture as a whole, so that even those artists who lacked any commitment to 'pop' proper, like Rauschenberg and Johns who preceded it, or Robbe-Grillet, or Stockhausen, were nevertheless willing to incorporate in their work popular images or erotic stereotypes or musical commonplaces which provided a direct link with an audience, even when these very elements were at the same time subjected to highly sophisticated formal procedures.

We thus find all the arts poised between theoretical rigour and eclecticism. In music, there is a tension between those who believe in an inevitable and logical progress based upon considerations entirely internal to the art, like Messiaen and Boulez, and those who became, after a rigorous beginning, much more eclectic, like Stockhausen and Berio. The symptom of this eclecticism is often indeed a direct confrontation with popular expression, as in Stockhausen's *Hymnen*, Cage's *Variations IV*, Berio's *Sinfonia* and *Cries of London*, Maxwell Davies's *St. Thomas Wake Foxtrot*, Henze's Sixth Symphony and *Tristan* (and even Tippett's Third Symphony, which is admittedly not advanced in idiom, but ends with a blues).

The situation in literature is rather different, since its avant-garde is not as dominant as it is in music and painting. Avant-garde writing is in many ways marginal to the mainstream, which is either conservatively realist or content with the techniques it has inherited from modernism. Thus there are plenty of writers in the period—all American—like Olson, Dorn, Lowell, and Berryman among poets, who are indeed experimental but do not pose those radical problems of language technique and interpretation which have been our chief concern here. Indeed my list of writers who are radically experimental—Beckett, Burroughs, and the new novelists—has been a short one. (Concrete poetry has perhaps unfairly been omitted from consideration.) And yet I feel that even here experimental writing has often been most effective when it has incorporated popular content; in Robbe-Grillet in ways we have already discussed, and, once more in America, in writers like Richard Brautigan, Robert Coover, Raymond Federman, Leonard Michaels, Thomas Pynchon, Ronald Sukenick, and Donald Barthelme, who is one of the most prolifically entertaining of this group.

Barthelme's work, although it is always meant to be read as fictional text, concentrates upon that fantastic dream-like metamorphosis of everyday reality which freedom from continuous narration licenses. Thus in his novel *Snow White* (1967), the marvellous of fairy tale is grafted on to the contemporary, with in-flight movies in shower stalls, pornographic pastry, and a heroine who has six beauty spots all in a row, writes a 'dirty great poem four pages long', fears 'MIRRORS/APPLES/POISONED COMBS' (none of which actually feature in her story) and spends three days at her psychiatrist's, to the deep suspicion of the dwarfs, who are the seven men whose apartment she lives in and cleans. (They wash windows and make Chinese baby food in vats for a living.) Her possible prince, Paul, is a part-time monk, hard edge painter, and ultimately spy, who, when he sees her black hair hanging from the window of the Employment Office, fears that 'some innocent person might come along, and see it, and conceive it his duty to climb up'.[9]

The story has thus been brought into a peculiarly satirical relationship with contemporary society, without losing in any way its fantastic qualities. Thus the seven men eat their 'Fear', 'Chix', and 'Rats' cereals, Snow White quotes Chairman Mao and wears 'heavy blue bulky shapeless quilted Peoples Volunteer trousers rather than the tight tremendous how-the-west-was-won trousers she formerly wore'.[10] Of course the everyday world will fail Snow White, as it is bound to do, for it has no place for sentimental fairy tale narratives. It is not even 'able to supply a prince' or 'civilised enough to supply the correct ending to the story'.[11] As one of the dwarfs, Clem, observes, 'Egalitarianism precludes princeliness'.[12] In all his work, Barthelme makes us feel with the dwarf Bill, that 'nourishment is refined from the ongoing circus of the mind in motion',[13] one which catches up within itself a fair amount of *dreck*, defined here as 'matter which presents itself as not wholly relevant (or indeed, at all relevant) but which, carefully attended to, can supply a kind of "sense" of what is going on'.[14] For like so many of his contemporaries, Barthelme imposes his characters' isolated and fragmentary fantasies upon the most junky parts of American experience. His narrative, like Pop collage, will assimilate almost anything. All the detritus of modern life is here, but it is made strange by being fragmented, for the narrative omits all those links by which we keep things in their places, both physical and logical, in order to control our real and our imagined environments. The result, as Barthelme puts it, is that 'The reader is not listening to an authoritative account of the world delivered by an expert (Faulkner on Mississippi or Hemingway on the corrida) but bumping into something that is there, like a rock or a refrigerator.'[15]

I would argue that eclectic work of this kind is in a perfectly obvious way the most central to the culture of the period we have been discussing, since it attempts to reconcile so many of its elements without compromising in matters of technique. In comparison the Zen-like jokes of Cage, the inferno despair of Beckett, the austere abstractions of Newman, and the strict serialism of Boulez seem marginal to the culture at large because they are so extreme, though of course they are the more satisfying to purists and élitists. To treat these artists as central would be like moving Artaud, Kafka, Webern, and Mondrian to a central position in modernism, which is one which, even if they were intellectually and technically of the highest importance, they did not in fact occupy. This is easily seen if we stop to compare them with the once more, confidently eclectic figures of Picasso, Stravinsky, and Eliot.

Ultimately the dominance of avant-garde movements and indeed of the figures within them will depend upon just that sense of historical perspective I have just applied to modernism, and so my remarks above are admittedly both speculative and polemical. The test for all such movements lies in their breaking away from traditional conventions in their beginnings, and establishing new ones. In their attempts to do this, all postmodern artists benefited from modernism in one important respect. For all the movements we have discussed, eclectic or extremist, have gained their prominence largely because one of the legacies of modernism was the *acceptability* of experimental art.

The days when a work like Schoenberg's *Verklärte Nacht* could be rejected because it contained a single uncatalogued dissonance ($B^\flat$—$A^\flat$—$E^\flat$—$G^\flat$—C—$E^\flat$) are gone. There is no longer a closed society, or a common language for that society, which can prompt a conservative resistance to experimental art. Even the silliest artistic idea seems to be accepted instantly by artistic institutions. Indeed the insistence upon the 'idea' so typical of avant-garde thinking, rather than upon traditional craftsmanship, seems to have made it difficult to distinguish between art and non-art, artist and non-artist, between simply doing your own thing and the production of an enduring object (as we saw in the case of conceptual art). Many such activities were difficult to classify as art in the traditional sense, and the status of their performers as artists derived simply from self-assertion, publicity, and institutional support. Similar confusions arose in experimental music, for instance in the Fluxus group, which aimed at 'the non structural and non theatrical qualities of the simple natural event, a game or a gag. It is the fusion of Spike Jones, Vaudeville, gag, children's games and Duchamp',[16] and in Cornelius Cardew's Scratch Orchestra, not entirely composed of professional musicians, which was defined in its constitution as 'a large number of enthusiasts pooling their resources (not primarily material resources) and assembling for action (music making, performance, edification).'[17]

It is in this essentially egalitarian and anarchic context of avant-garde activity that purely gratuitous actions and objects achieved a certain acceptability. It is difficult to explain otherwise the ubiquity of works like John McCracken's red painted board, leaning against a wall, which showed up in so many galleries, and whose title in the New York Museum of Modern Art, 'Art of the Real' Show was, very appropriately, *There is no reason not to*. However minimal this work may be, and however much it may seem to ask the question, 'What is the difference between painting and sculpture?' it is still very silly. And even if this particular piece may be thought to have done its work by provoking the critical rage of the previous sentence, my main point still stands, if one remembers that there were so *many* equally 'acceptable' objects like it at the time that their provocation simply became an irritant, easily dissolved in indifference by any person of intelligence.

The institutional acceptance of such works of art may well seem to stem from the fact that the majority has no intellectually respectable culture of its own and no major figures of the present to counterpose to the adversary experimental culture. But it is simply not true to say that in consequence 'bourgeois culture' is shattered, since it is this culture rather than any other that supports and in particular pays for avant-garde art, and it has in fact been immensely hospitable to experiment from modernism on. It is rather the case

that there is now a very large class of persons who are
receptive for one reason or another to experimental art, 'an
audience large enough to sustain a world of cultural production on its own . . . those persons in the knowledge and
communications industries who, with their families, would
number several million persons'.[18] This cultural mass is not
conservative in the old sense. Its educational experience and
its appetite for novelty, partly derived from the mass media,
make it expect new art to be extreme, and even adversary to
its own culture, in so far as that is technologically well-
served, liberal, comfortable, and thus guilt-inducing. We
must remember too that this highly educated élite can also
rely upon enjoying the art of the past in museums and
through books and gramophone records to an extent never
before known, and can thus easily afford to tolerate an
avant-garde which provides the more extreme part of their
experience. Thus modernism both forces the contemporary
artist to stylistic extremes, and provides his audience with a
pleasurable means of retreat from his product (a situation
neatly symbolized by those concert programmes which
sandwich a contemporary work between Debussy and
Stravinsky). After all, although avant-garde activity has
always had an extreme air of commitment among its creators
and immediate adherents, its general public is by definition
more at home in the established part of the culture.

All this makes the traditional adversary and subversive
roles of the avant-garde rather more difficult to sustain; a
kind of repressive tolerance obtains, even if there are occasional outbursts in the lower-brow newspapers over government support for artists who sit on poles in shopping
centres, or knock down walls with their heads, or walk round
the countryside balancing planks on them.

The notion of an avant-garde which attacked 'the
bourgeoisie' and thus refused to see itself as the reflection of
an underlying social structure was common in Europe just
before and after the First World War. One can see surrealism as a genuinely adversary movement, moved by the two
radical ideologies invented by the moderns, Marxism and
psycho-analysis. But recent avant-garde movements lack

such radically disturbing ideological perspectives, and in any case have had a much more stable society to contend with. Thus Breton's exhortation to us in his second surrealist manifesto to remember 'that the primary aim of all Dada spectacles has always been to cause the greatest possible confusion and that in the minds of its organisers it was nothing so much as creating the highest pitch of misunderstanding between performer and audience' was happily rather than discomfortingly achieved in those 'happenings' and environments of the 1960s which so directly exploited the Dada and surrealist traditions, as in Jim Dine's *The Car Crash* (1960) or more gently in Alen Kaprow's *Fluids* (1967)—'during three days, about twenty rectangular enclosures of ice blocks . . . are built throughout the city. Their walls are unbroken. They are left to melt.'

Indeed we rather like the anxiety caused in us by avant-garde art. It seems to be an entertaining source both of social criticism, and in consequence, of a rather self-congratulatory sense of our social freedom. Hence the phenomenon of the anti-bourgeois bourgeois, who accepts society more or less as it is, while at the same time entertaining a set of intellectual and artistic notions which are contradicted by his actual behaviour. As John Weightman points out in discussing this phenomenon, this is hardly surprising, since after all there was Christianity but there was also sin. He cites as an example Jean Genet's *Les Paravents*, 'a powerful and nihilistic denunciation of French society, which was brilliantly staged by the French National Theatre. This was an almost perfect example of society applauding its own negation.'[19] Tom Wolfe's famous essay on 'radical chic' develops this theme.

Aesthetic subversion has thus become revolutionary pantomime. The institutions which tolerate these latter-day manifestations have given them an almost fictional status, and attempts at outrage or 'consciousness-raising' have become dramatic events. For example, Mr Jean Toche, who was arrested at the instigation of the Museum of Modern Art in New York for mailing an open letter urging the kidnapping of museum trustees and officials. His 'genre' as an artist was proclaimed to be the composing of such manifestos and letters of protest. He had accused the museum of vandalism because it *removed* an inscription sprayed by a visitor upon *Guernica*, and wanted those responsible to be tried in a 'People's Court'. This is, as Harold Rosenberg says, a burlesque of avant-garde radicalism and a plagiarism of Dada, but Toche nevertheless received the support of 100 artists, art teachers, critics, curators, historians, dealers, and collectors who denounced 'the political arrest of artist Jean Toche' and affirmed his right to 'freedom of artistic expression'.[20] Here the ambivalence between 'really meaning it' (that trustees should be kidnapped) and the fictional manifesto is neatly echoed by the equally ambivalent and fantasizing bad faith of those who could persuade themselves that his arrest was 'politically' inspired.

Even the most ideological literature is in no better case, whether it be Burroughs and his paranoiac fantasies, or the new novelist seeking revolution through the disruption of the 'bourgeois order' of language, since the adversary culture these writers represent is institutionalized and neutralized by its academic acceptance. Indeed it is characteristic of this type of 'revolution' that it confuses and reverses the roles of art and action. The prerequisite of revolution is a revolution of language, say the *Tel Quel* group in France; conventional discourse and its prevailing ideology must be abolished. Thus a multipolar, de-hierarchized text, like that of many new novels, with no unitary mimetic sense, is thought to be an indirect attack upon such subordinating political notions as monotheism, monarchy, imperialism, and so on.[21] But this is to confuse a mere analogy with cause and effect.[22] It is difficult to see how such reorganization on the artistic level can have much effect on the larger political one; it is rather like hoping that the growth of Esperanto will abolish Romanian and French. The idea of reforming language itself is certainly a radical one, but it puts the political commitments of literature at a considerable remove from that direct engagement with ideology based upon realism found in Sartre and Camus, and against which so many French writers and critics are in fact reacting. (That ideological conflict can *still* be described within conventional language and upon realist assumptions is amply demonstrated by that tradition in the American novel which shows a hero pitted against a hostile society which tries to condition him; hence Ellison's *Invisible Man*, Heller's *Catch-22*, Kesey's *One Flew Over the Cuckoo's Nest*, and even Pynchon's *The Crying of Lot 49.*)

This is not of course to deny that the *implicit* criticism of language and its ideological codes in the work of writers like Robbe-Grillet, who reveal the junk in the sub-conscious lumber-room of society, or indeed the wholly explicit attacks of Barthes, Kristeva, Althusser, Macherey, and others is of value. It is simply paradoxical that the abolition of the realistic mode might be thought to dismiss the serious or the tragic, which are the traditional allies of ideological opposition, and to leave us free to 'play' with language. As critics like Derrida would have it, the absence of ultimate meanings opens an unbounded space for the play of signification. One might doubt of course whether our sense of the tragic, or indeed of the 'transcendental signifier' can be thus easily abolished. It is a typical move within left-wing ideology to pretend that after *this* (ideological move), *that* (generally accepted practice) is 'no longer possible'. Such pretensions are really only possible within tightly knit groups with a strong sense of hierarchy and vigorous powers of excommunication, characteristics which are hardly liberating.

A certain primal innocence may nevertheless be discovered in such anti-bourgeois writers; the ludic novels of Robbe-Grillet and the exploration of inner space in Burroughs are games with inverted values, rather in the sense that de Sade's or Pauline Réage's encyclopaedic listings and combinations of sexual possibilities are games in which, as we saw, repetition and disorientation of form ultimately neutralizes any emotional or moral response we may have to the content of the work.

Thus the arguments for this type of writing have a certain intellectual appeal, since the attack on idealism, moral absolutes, or the empirical liberalism implicit in realism, has a satisfying traditional philosophical cast. But the claims for the *social* effectiveness of such works will always seem negligible, in proportion to the narrowness of their institutional base, since the dominant ideology they rightfully attack has by definition bigger (or at least better distributed) weapons, like Harold Robbins, Jacqueline Susann, television soap-opera, and so on.

II

The two aspects of the avant-garde I have emphasized, its acceptability, and hence the frequent neutralization of its adversary gestures, are reinforced by the simple speed of change within experimental art. For example, we have in earlier chapters been implicitly much concerned with the evolution of art in America, in discussing the work of Pollock, Newman, Stella, André, LeWitt, Johns, Rauschenberg, and others. In the period thus covered one might guess that a new style has managed to establish itself there every two or three years, in the rough sequence: abstract expressionism—post-painterly abstraction (hard edge and colour field)—kinetic and Op art—Pop art and assemblage—environments and happenings—Minimalism, conceptualism, and documentary art—and photorealism. These movements have all been echoed or anticipated in Britain, France, and Germany. (Though one might note that England's chief contribution apart from Pop seems to have been the sustained painting of the figure, through Sutherland, Bratby, Frank Auerbach, Lucien Freud, Bacon, Hockney, and the expatriate American, Kitaj.) This extreme stylistic mobility of course reflects not only artistic eclecticism and critical trend-spotting, but also the buoyancy of the avant-garde market in art, and the fact that an artist's discoveries may be published throughout the world in art magazines almost as soon as he is exhibited. Mass-media technology eliminates cultural time-lag.

The result is that examples of each style seem worth acquiring, as genuine even if ephemeral pieces of instant art history, which in postmodern terms means any work of art backed up by widely disseminated critical publicity. The art which we recognize as avant-garde may thus lull us into accepting sheer novelty of experience without, immediately at least, raising questions of value. In a consumer society the serious and the trivial alike profit by being new. We are, for example, newly confronted by two paintings with a ladder between them, or the artist's bed daubed in paint and suspended against the wall, or by a drawer stuck in the middle of a canvas. [23] There is little doubt that these works challenge our previous experience of 'painting' and thus constitute a gesture within the history of art, but we may have very little idea whether the gesture is a worthwhile one. Like other products, such works can only ultimately by judged in the perspective of time. Some are hula hoops, some are skateboards, some are three-dimensional cinema, some have come to stay. Such art may simply be used up, like so much bad pop painting, which was no better than the advertisements from which it was derived; or like Duchamp's urinal, it may somehow manage to survive simply as an example; or, exceptionally, it may be a permanent and enriching addition to our 'musées imaginaires'.

This speed of change and profusion was largely abetted by what I have earlier called pedagogical intervention and theory dominance, particularly within the newly growing art schools. Thus the artist may submit himself to working rules that may prevent him from imitating the past, or invent rules unique to each work, so that the notion of convention itself is attacked, and so on. These essentially critical decisions, it is often grandiosely claimed (by Stockhausen, by Robbe-Grillet, by Stella), mark turning-points in the history of art; and a new 'science' of composition, of 'écriture', or of plastic construction is revealed. The work of art simultaneously breaks previous codes and reveals new ones, whose logic we are expected to grasp in order to appreciate it. Anecdote generates anecdote, music expands like a galaxy, cubes multiply with cubes, a map is no longer a map, a mirror no longer a mirror, 'temporal space' accepts whatever noises happen to be around, and so on.

This essentially critical context for artistic production works in two ways. It can as we have seen provide a framework for the major artist. There is no doubt that the work of Cage, Boulez, and Stockhausen largely stems from their respectively dominating *idées fixes*, Boulez perhaps trapped within the serialist aesthetic, Cage always seeming original through chance and Dadaist display, and Stockhausen endlessly prolific of frequently half-baked theories which nevertheless lead to a seemingly equally endless number of changes in compositional procedure, from the Webernian pointillism of *Kontra-Punkte* to the massive collage of *Hymnen*. Theory and epistemology in all these cases have begotten art, even when the epistemology is hopelessly misunderstood, as for example in comparisons between minimalist art and linguistics or Stockhausen's justification of his procedures by reference to the concepts and terminology of modern physics.[24]

The outcome of such theoretically inspired investigations may of course be highly unpredictable. In other cases, like that of André, the result of the application of theory is only too easily anticipated. The test of all such theories for an audience is, as we shall see, the intelligibility and the effect of the work of art, but for the artist it may have a different function, for he may be relatively indifferent to aesthetic effect and confine his ambitions to the making of a distinct move within avant-garde theory.

Theory dominance may thus work on a number of different levels. On the lower ones it allowed artists and their critics to welcome minor theoretically sanctioned manœuvres as though they were great artistic discoveries. For this type of minimal avant-gardism all that is required is a strong critical context. For example, the key term, as it arose out of abstract expressionism, was 'flatness'—'flatness, two-dimensionality was the only consideration shared with no other art, and so modernist painting oriented itself to flatness.'[25] Jasper Johns's targets were 'flat', as were his flags and number paintings, and so despite their grim Dadaism they were to some degree acceptable to critics. Indeed Tom Wolfe has written a brilliant satire on the New York critical establishment, and its three bergs—Greenberg, Rosenberg, and Steinberg, which emphasizes this theme.[26] These essentially formalist criteria, which, as we have argued, put verbal formulations between the spectator and the work, were unfortunately dominant in the criticism of the fifties and early sixties, so that the placing of stripes, the merging of colour into ground, consideration of the whole field of the picture plane, and the solving of 'problems' within it often led to a sterile pattern-making, the search for a holistic, recognizable, and marketable design.[27] Questions of response and general significance tended to be ignored. Hence the rather tart comment of Harold Rosenberg that Stella, as a painter formed almost exclusively in the practice of abstract art, thus 'stopped dealing with nature and imagination and devoted himself entirely to problems'.[28] This judgement, though hardly fair to Stella, points to a situation in which much of the emotional expressivity of earlier abstract art was lost, in the exploration of relatively minor formal problems dictated by the history of art. Hence also Patrick Heron's engagingly enthusiastic description of his apparently epoch-making decision to make his strokes go right to the edges of the canvas:

In early 1957, feeling, I think, that the allover emphasis and the uniform looseness and the too-mechanical scribbles of what the French called Tachism and the Americans Action Painting needed to be harnessed slightly more rigidly again to the edges of the canvas, I allowed my arm to extend a number of these vertical brushstrokes until they made contact with the top and bottom edges of the canvas, *Scarlet Verticals; March 1957* is an example . . . It was therefore a natural step—and a very short one—to proceed from this painting to canvasses whose total image consisted solely of these long vertical strokes, in differing colours, all reaching more or less from top to bottom of the picture format . . . Although these were the first striped paintings to be painted anywhere, I was unaware at the time of having invented a new pictorial formula: something called a 'colour stripe painting' did not exist at the time, even as a concept.[29]

It is in the light of this formalism in abstract painting that the conceptualist and minimalist schools can be seen to have marked the inevitable triumph of theory over art.

Similarly minimal avant-garde manœuvres are found in literature, which has occasionally adopted simple game-like combinatory procedures reminiscent of the work of André and LeWitt. For example, in Edwin Morgan's intriguing permutation of the letters in the sentence 'il faut être absolument moderne' to make newspaper headlines, and in much other constructivist concrete poetry, which 'results from an arrangement of materials according to a scheme or system set up by the poet which must be adhered to on its own terms (permutational poems)'.[30] An extreme example is Emmett Williams's long kinetic sequence *Sweethearts*, which is constructed entirely from that word's eleven letters in their original order, and in which no single poem can be more than eleven letters wide or eleven letters deep.

Such techniques can release the writer from many of the traditional burdens of personal choice and self-expression, and like much formulaic painting (particularly of the 'op' and kinetic schools) rely upon a painstaking ingenuity. Even more self-conscious and more critically aware in the bad academic sense, is that work which John Barth has appropriately enough called 'The Literature of Exhaustion', of which he himself has produced a fair number of examples. Here the manipulations of Nabokov, Borges, and others simply become overt as the author comments on his own procedures in a perpetual *mise-en-abîme*. Thus Barth's own 'Autobiography', 'Life Story' and 'Title' in his *Lost in the Funhouse* collection (1968) all refer to their own process of writing or implied performance. They are supposed to have a cumulative effect in series, as the funhouse of fiction reveals its own intricate, yet tatty and illusory internal workings, in a kind of Coney Island of the creative mind: the extract which follows can only dimly suggest the complexities of the whole.

What's new?   Nothing.
Conventional startling opener.   Sorry if I'm interrupting the Progress of Literature, she said, in a tone that adjective clause suggesting good-humoured irony but in fact defensively and imperfectly masking a taunt.   The conflict is established though as yet unclear in detail.   Standard conflict.   Let's skip particulars.   What do you want from me?   What'll be the story this time?   Same old story.   Just thought I'd see if you were still

around. Before. What? Quit right here. Too late. Can't we start over? What's past is past. On the contrary, what's forever past is eternally present. The future? Blank. All this is just fill in. Hang on.[31]

Barth warns us in his Author's Note that this piece called 'Title' is a 'triply schizoid monologue' which 'addresses itself simultaneously to three matters: the "Author's" difficulties with his companion, his analogous difficulties with the story he's in the process of composing, and the not dissimilar straits in which, I think, mistakenly, he imagines his culture and its literature to be'. This is a fairly heavy burden for this rather flat and often sub-Beckettian prose to bear; and one may wonder whether this critical game-playing is not basically misconceived. We are really being asked to disentangle a complex metaphorical allegory of the creative process, and may feel that this type of story (as opposed to the brilliant 'Ambrose his Mark' and 'Lost in the Funhouse' of the same volume) isn't really about anything much, and that in Richard Poirier's pungent phrase, its 'relation to the possibilities of literature is like the relation of a good cookbook to food'.[32]

Work like this may be sophomorically flattering in its rationalism and disturbing in its superficial promptings towards the classroom skills of practical criticism. Like the other forms of conceptual art which we discussed earlier, it very much needs reinforcement by other values such as humour, satire, or serious mimetic commitment. These qualities are achieved I think by a number of the American writers I cited earlier, particularly Robert Coover, whose 'The Magic Poker' and 'The Baby Sitter' achieve all that many new novelists do technically and adds to this a really disturbing mythical and emotional overtone.[33]

But work of this distinction is rare. The game-playing aspects of literature all too frequently reflect a turning away from those deeper responsibilities which have traditionally been seen in moral terms. The concentration upon the second-order matters of mode of discourse and of theoretically analysable linguistic structures has diminished commitment to mimesis and hence to content. Any materials will do. (Avant-garde writing is thus in the starkest of contrasts to the liberal tradition in literature, which is still sustained in America by Bellow and Roth, in England by Wilson and Murdoch, and in France by Bazin and Rochefort.) Even reportorial or non-fiction novels, whose subject-matter positively dictates a moral significance, play with their own fictionality, as in Mailer's *Armies of the Night*, Vonnegut's *Slaughterhouse Five*, or Capote's *In Cold Blood*; the uncertainties they display concerning facts do just as much to cast doubt upon their seriousness as to express it. The creative mind thus triumphs over its materials in a way which deliberately licenses lying or amnesia at the same time as it offers us the pleasures of fictional form, often enough as a substitute for that direct confrontation with substantive issues that Sartre had so strongly advocated at the beginning of our period in his 'What is Literature?'.

The avant-garde thus presents the confusing picture one would expect in a diversely experimental situation; but I feel that some central points emerge. The most important perhaps is this. Despite the well-known fact that the celebrated artist of one era may be almost wholly neglected in the next, the converse rarely holds; we *do* know who the major artists of the postmodern period are, and it is thus possible to come to terms to some degree with our own times. Thus we concluded that from austere and reductive beginnings, contemporary art has broadened out to a state in which there are a number of competing styles operating at varying levels of engagement with society, often in a mood of acceptance that gives the lie to those who might believe that compared with modernist art, postmodern art lacks confidence. All the styles we have discussed may indeed have their sources and parallels in the pre-war period, but these have usually been adapted in a way that leaves most art instantly recognizable as contemporary. Thus although I have earlier compared Stella with Kupka and Delaunay, Robbe-Grillet with early Beckett, Judd with the Bauhaus, Berio's vocal works with *Erwartung*, Messiaen's and Ligeti's impressionism with that of Debussy, Johns with Duchamp, Newman with Mondrian, and so on, I do not think that such parallels do much to show that postmodern art is just a late phase of modernism. The attempt to prove that everything has been done before can indeed advertise a scholarly ingenuity in digging out similarities, but it would do little to display the unique over-all shape of contemporary culture.

On the other hand, this culture now seems to deny any very powerful ideological functions to art. There is nothing in the contemporary period to parallel the political commitments of the naturalist or existentialist novel, or the psychoanalytic insights of writers like Lawrence, Auden, and the surrealists. It is perhaps in the light of this withdrawal from the commitment so much discussed by existentialists at the beginning of our period that much contemporary art can be seen to be tied to the internal processes of its own techniques and the critical or aesthetic theory that justifies it. There is thus a sense in which contemporary art is autonomous as it never was before. Its willingness to leave the overpowering complexities of society to journalists, sociologists, economists, television producers, and even, by implication, politicians, in favour of an involvement with its own logical or absurdist theory has resulted in a new aestheticism; a revival of art for art's sake directed either to extremely personal and passive types of psychological response, or to essentially critical ones. It is to a consideration of these effects of art that I now turn.

Chapter Five: The Experience of the Work of Art

Statement of aesthetic withdrawal
The undersigned, Robert Morris, being the maker of the metal
construction entitled Litanies, described in the Annexe exhibit A
hereby withdraws from said construction all aesthetic quality and
control and declares that from the date thereof said construct has
no such content. Dated November 15th, 1953.

Si l'on recherchait dans un Klee ou un Mirò ce que l'on peut voir
dans un tableau de Véronèse ou de Poussin . . . alors Klee ou Mirò
seraient . . . bien 'difficiles à lire'.
Claude Simon

The challenge of experimental art lies not simply in the fact
that it exploits new techniques, but in its demanding a new
type of response. It is this psychological readjustment that
can be most difficult to achieve. In what follows I wish to
discuss the effects of the art we have looked at earlier, drawing together some of the themes of our previous argument
and introducing some new examples to reinforce it.

Before we can experience art we have to locate its object as
the locus of all its values. This has never been too difficult in
the case of literature, whose medium has remained at least as
stable as the language which expresses it, and once we reach
the borderline, in concrete poetry, we could always say that
literature has become visual art. But the other postmodern
arts often make any such object difficult to find; it may
migrate across categories, be metamorphosed from one performance to another, or be a mere event, whose aim is to
leave a fading concept in the memory.

Music has been particularly unstable in this respect, varying as it does from fully notated scores of the traditional type
to graphic and text scores which allow for any member of
realizations. The relationship between notional work or
'score' and performance has thus become much looser. Even
fully notated music may be so complex that no performer
could manage it accurately; and the growth of chance
methods of composition and of indeterminacy (performer
choice and improvisation) has opened this gap still further.
Thus a performance of *Klavierstück XI*, or Ligeti's *Volumina* for
organ, or Christian Wolff's *Duo II* for pianists (1958) (which

may be five or fifteen minutes long), is not simply one particular interpretation of a notional ideal work like a Beethoven piano sonata, but may involve a radical rearrangement of content. Some graphic scores indeed, like the abstract art and mobiles which frequently inspire them (particularly in the work of Earle Brown), are often no more than carefully selected stimuli for improvisation. One might almost as well 'play' a Mondrian. Works like these are very largely indeterminate, but they do usually preserve some conventional relationships between the performer, traditional instruments, and notated directions. It has of course been the aim of the conceptualists to disturb and devalue these categories still further, to the point at which, in Nyman's words, there is little more left than 'a *situation* in which sounds may occur, a *process* of generating action (sounding or otherwise), and a *field* delineated by certain compositional rules'.[1]

For example, John Cage's *0' 0"* (1962) is supposed to be nothing more specific than the maximum amplification with no feedback of a disciplined action. No interruptions are allowed; no two performances are to be of the same action, nor may the action be the performance of a musical composition. In one realization Cage tied a microphone round his neck, turned up the amplification, and drank a glass of water. This sounded like 'the pounding of giant surf'. In this kind of work the actions performed are often of no particular significance in themselves, and are wholly parasitic upon their audience's willingness to maintain conventional expectations even when they know they will be defeated yet again, as also for example in George Brecht's *Comb Music* (comb event, 1959) which involves holding a comb in one hand and running a thumb or finger-nail over the ends of each prong, or his *Piano Music* (1962) which involves placing a vase of flowers upon a piano. Although such art may seem to cross aesthetic categories (noise or gesture become 'music', just as a pile of rubbish may be 'sculpture') it actually exudes contempt for serious art, and a fear of the incapacity to produce it. The most one can say for it is that it is symptomatic of a situation we find also in the visual arts, in which *anything* can be accepted as art from masterpieces of the traditional kind like Bacon's Triptychs to the junk sculptures of Robert Morris and others. Anarchy and self-congratulation join hands in these futile gestures.

In both these arts, the nearer we approach this lower end of the spectrum (and I have spared the reader many of the examples to be found in the literature), the more we need the artist's activity recognized as such to 'define' art for us. As I have argued earlier, once we have adopted this excessively liberal attitude, we have little choice in the matter. Andy Warhol has publicized such issues throughout his career. Thus he asserts that his film *Chelsea Girls* is art because 'first of all it was made by an artist, and second that would come out as art',[2] and in 1966 he announced in a newspaper that he would sign anything brought to him, including currency, the value of which he now had the power to increase by turning it into a 'work of art' by Andy Warhol.

The publicity accorded an artist's career may thus be in inverse proportion to the significance of the actual performance or aesthetic object he produces. It takes a Warhol or a Cage to get away with $0'\ 0''$, or painted Brillo boxes or pictures of soup-cans and Coke bottles as art, and to establish them as representative of an aesthetic trend. This was in fact much disapproved of by the artist to whom it is chiefly indebted, Marcel Duchamp:

This neo-Dada, which they call New Realism, Pop Art, assemblage, etc. is an easy way out, and lives on what Dada did. When I discovered ready-mades I thought to discourage aesthetics. In neo-Dada they have taken my ready-mades and found aesthetic beauty in them. I threw the bottle rack and the urinal in their faces for a challenge and now they admire them for their aesthetic beauty.[3]

Of course the objects Duchamp attacks here are often transformed by art rather more than his ready-mades were; for example the bronze flashlights and beer-cans of Johns, who remarks of the latter, 'somebody told me that Bill de Kooning said of Leo Castelli that you could give that sonofabitch two beer-cans and he could sell them. I thought, what a wonderful idea for a sculpture.'[4] Works like these, and Oldenberg's *Soft Mayonnaise* (1964), or *Giant Gym Shoes* (1963), or Christo's *Wrapped Bottle* (1958), make fun of the idea that museums should contain treasures to contemplate, but they are really no more than surrealist objects with the shock removed.

They also blur the distinction between art and reality, and this has been a major theme of the visual arts in the post-modern period, from abstract works whose large scale made it possible for them to constitute the complete visual field of the beholder in a tradition descending from Monet, to three-dimensional environments like those of Dine and Kienholz, which descend from the Merzbauen of Schwitters. This play with the distinction between the work of art and the larger environment, in Stockhausen's House of Music, and the dramatic 'happening', as well as in the visual arts, has been useful, I think, in releasing that type of response which makes us look at our own surroundings from a different point of view. As Wilde remarked, London's fogs were entirely a creation of the impressionists, and even minimalist art can help to sharpen our attitude to the often equally minimalist architectural forms of the modern city. This play between artifice and reality means that art crosses conceptual boundaries, in many cases with a witty effect, as in Rauschenberg's *Pilgrim* (1960) in which a painted stripe continues downward over a chair placed against the painting, or his *Winter Pool* (1959) with its ladder between two paintings, or most notoriously the paint-soaked *Bed* (1955) from his own studio. On a larger scale, we may have works which confuse painting with the spectator's own space, as in some of Wesselman's *Great American Nudes*, where real carpeting may run up to the painted figure framed by shower curtains and a real telephone on the wall may ring from time to time. In works like this traditional forms of artistic illusion and everyday objects are put into a juxtaposition which is often ironic. Thus Oldenburg's *Bedroom Ensemble I* (1963) contains rhomboidal bits of furniture, so that all their angles are in false perspective, to disconcertingly nightmarish effect; this is further emphasized by false textures, for the sheets on the bed are made of shiny white vinyl and the bedspread is quilted black plastic. Oldenburg says that his bedroom 'might have been called composition for (rhomboids) columns and discs . . . my grey little geometric home in the west, is two-stepping with Edward Hopper . . . All the fun is locking horns with impossibilities—for example combining our notions of sculpture with our notions of a single "vulgar" object: hamburger or bedroom.'[5][See Pls. 12 and 13.]

Equally disturbing but also comic are works like Kienholz's *Art Show*, in which grotesque models of spectators stand about a room, burbling unintelligible rubbish through their grille-like mouths, powered by the tape-recorders inside them. We, the 'real' flesh-and-blood spectators, press a button and out it comes. As there are pictures on the walls too, at which *we* look and to which we respond, our gestures and attitudes and more particularly anything we say seem to be parodied by the models. It is a peculiarly inhibiting experience, since the pictures are of the kind that may or may not merit the models' gibberish.

The artistic object both becomes and modifies the natural as opposed to human environment in an absurdly ambitious and radical way in the work of Christo; for instance when he uses a million square feet of polythene and thirty-five miles of rope to cover (or as he puts it to 'wrap') a mile of Australian coastline. Here nature is made artificial and turned into art; as it is also in 'earth art', which may be very grand, as in Robert Smithson's *Spiral Jetty* (1970) in the Great Salt Lake, Utah, or very trivial, as in Peter Hutchinson's creation of a ring of fungus where none would normally grow, by placing bread round the top of a volcano in Mexico.

II

Many of the works we have been discussing thus depend upon a kind of confusion of art and environment in which both are thereby 'made strange'. They are embedded in reality, but also divorced from it by the artist's activity. They are self-contradictions woven round sounds or objects or situations we have encountered in other contexts. In some cases, for example Cage's water drinking or Warhol's Brillo boxes, there may be the smallest hair-line difference between the two. Our mental set is neatly disrupted, and we have to work upon two planes at once, as when documentary suddenly becomes fiction or vice versa, as often happens in Norman Mailer. But there is an entirely opposite tendency in post-modern art to enforce a peculiarly exclusive attention to its object; to abjure any mimetic commitments, any correspondence even with the everyday life of the emotions.

Purely abstract paintings which may form an environment but don't necessarily reflect it, most obviously call for this kind of response, which was aimed at by many abstract expressionists, as the following *cri de cœur* from Gottlieb shows: 'I frequently hear the question, "what do these paintings mean?" This is simply the wrong question. Visual images do not have to conform to either verbal thinking or optical facts. A better question would be "Do these images convey any emotional truth?".'[6]

Abstract painting is thus most in flight from interpretation, having no obviously mimetic content in which to base it, and so provoking no settled language in which we can describe our emotional responses. It not only demands the observer's exclusive attention but isolates him. Its effects are thus much less palpable than, for example, those feelings of horror we may derive from the agonized distortions of the human which we find in the work of Francis Bacon, who, incidentally, believes that in abstract art 'there is nothing other than the aesthetic of the painter and his few sensations . . . it can convey very watered down feelings because I think any shapes can. But I don't think it can convey feeling in the grand sense.'[7] One might of course urge against Bacon that much of the work of Pollock and Rothko does convey 'grand emotions' and that the feeling here is much more closely tied to the work of art, undistracted by those humanitarian feelings aroused by his own work and that of De Kooning; but the main point to establish, and simple introspection is all that will serve here, is that though the emotions caused by abstract painting may have very different bases in cause and belief, they nevertheless exist.

It has all the same to be admitted that many postmodern abstract works seem to have value on a rather lower, or cooler level, as intense complexes of sensation rather than anything else; like Morris Louis's flamelike 'Veils', they are essentially Paterian in intention and in effect. Thus at an extreme, as Marshall McLuhan notes, over-all black painting like Ad Reinhardt's seems to mark 'the obsolescence of eye culture' and call for 'a response of the central nervous system'. The physiology here may be shaky but the metaphor points to the blankness induced in us by the blank work.

More typically of course, we take pleasure in particular configurations, patterns, balances, and harmonic colour relationships. This gives rise to critical appraisals like the following (Rosenberg on Ellsworth Kelly) which is typical: 'he has the feeling of rightness of a first class designer, a fine sense of proportion, and satisfying juxtapositions of colours and of tones'.[8] Similar remarks can be applied to the whole of the central tradition of abstract painting since modernism, where design, proportion, and sensitivity to colour all combine to produce 'satisfaction'. What is interesting in the contemporary period is the way in which painters have sought the extremes about this central core. Thus any attempt at an over-all *Gestalt* is frustrated by Pollock but is supposed to be instantaneous in Noland; the complexities of relation and balance were scorned by Stella in his early work; and the implicit method of production of the abstract design claimed importance, in ways as different as the existentialist gesture of the abstract expressionist and the pre-compositional calculation of LeWitt.

Although abstract painting demands an exclusivity of attention by its very nature, it is also seen as an instance of a particular style; and the establishment of such a style, against which variations can be played, has been the chief concern of many postmodern artists. Abstract painting since the war has been dominated by the notion of the series suggested by the work of Mondrian and others; Motherwell's obsession with the design of ovals wedged in between vertical rectangles, Johns's targets and numbers, Noland's chevron series, Stella's black pin-stripe works and protractor works, and Bridget Riley's wave designs which co-vary with their optical effects. There are conventions here which facilitate comparison without ever becoming as simple or overt as the rules which we saw underlying André's series of modular sculptures. In the latter case we are being satisfied by the rules and their observance as much as by the work: this is an achievement of a vastly lower order than that of Mondrian, for example, who produced a large number of satisfying solutions to the arrangement of bars and rectangles, without ever, so far as one can tell, following any 'rules'.[9] The test of value here lies in the hard-won satisfactions of experience, rather than in any easy security of method.

As we noted earlier, the simplification involved in rule-governed work reflects a deliberate avoidance of complexity, of the balance and harmony provided by the modernist cubist aesthetic, so that as Stella noted, 'in the newer American painting we strive to get the thing in the middle, and symmetrical, but just to get a kind of force, just to get the thing on the canvas. The balance factor isn't important.'[10]

This simplification by subtraction is typical of the postmodern development away from modernism (and it applies just as much to the athematic atmospheric music of Ligeti and Lutoslawski as it does to the work by Pollock and Newman which we discussed at the outset). This progression reaches a dead end in the minimalist work of sculptors like André and Robert Morris, who was not surprised that such work was called 'negative, boring, nihilistic' and echoes Stella in blaming our knowledge of the past for this: 'these judgements arise from confronting the work with expectations structured by a cubist aesthetic in which what is to be had from the work is located strictly within the specific object'.[11] His demands here are as impossible as those of John Cage in urging us to forget Beethoven, for it is almost impossible for us to give up *haute cuisine* for an exclusive diet of rice and mushrooms; but they do remind us of the wholly particularist mental set which is necessary for the appreciation of much postmodern art.

One of the most demanding of artists, if we are to attempt to specify a response to this essentially simple type of work, is Mark Rothko. In his painting from 1950 on, the style of over-all figuration is repeated with little variation from canvas to canvas. The rectangle of the canvas is a one-colour ground visible along the edge of, and occasionally through, an opening between three or four horizontal blocks of colour with brushed surfaces and furry borders. These shapes are thus bled into their ground, fusing both into a single plane. It is then the *emotional* content of the work and not its design which varies, along with the line, weight, colour tone, expansion, and contraction of his oblongs of colour. These oblongs seem peculiarly immaterial and atmospheric, brooding and darkening to reddish-brown toward the end of his career. Their calm simplicity is completely antithetical to the unpredictable filling of the flat space in the action painting of Pollock or Kline, which seems psychologically so much more complex. It is an art like Mondrian's, which commands attention after nearly everything has been excluded (though not influenced by it: like Morris Louis, Rothko is more akin to Matisse and to his friend Milton Avery). The colour is purely atmospheric, passive, and recessive, almost self-effacing, and possibly ironic. Rothko's aim is thus paradoxically similar to Pollock's, in that: 'each seeks an absolute in which the receptive viewer can lose himself, the one in compulsive movement, the other in all pervading, as if internalised, sensation of a dominant colour'.[12] The blocks of colour both radiate an aura outwards and seem to veil what lies behind them. Their environmental size overwhelms the viewer and the hallucinatory uncertainty they thus generate echoes the unanalysable sublimity aimed at by Newman. Robert Rosenblum suggests that such painting is in some ways derived from the romantic landscape painting of Friedrich and Turner, its 'horizontal division echoing the primordial separation of earth and sky',[13] but such associations seem as unnecessary to these paintings as the linking of the work of Mondrian to canal patterns in Holland or of Newman to the Cabbalah. Rothko's aims were certainly as profound as those of his contemporaries. He was attempting to move beyond the mere hedonism of colour combination to a greater impressiveness, to the expression of 'the basic human emotions—tragedy, ecstacy, doom and so on. The people who weep before my pictures are having the same religious experience I had when I painted them.'[14] These are strong claims, and yet one can sense how this function might be performed if his paintings are seen in the cultural context which gains them the type of attention they seem to demand. Properly hung in museums they are immensely impressive, and even more so in the Rothko chapel in Houston, Texas, which was commissioned by Mr and Mrs John de Ménil.

Painting like Rothko's demands to be appreciated for its own sake. It has no obvious mimetic or instrumental relationship with the external world. If it facilitates withdrawal into a contemplative or even mystical state, then so much the better. Like Stockhausen's *Stimmung* and *Carré*, it pulsates but does not move, and its colour relations are used to define something mysterious which is purely internal to itself, in a perpetual search for a pure 'chord' of feeling. [See Pl. 14.]

III

The type of abstract art we have been discussing lies at an extreme from that didactic, theory-dominated art, which has made so large a part of avant-garde activity. It is essentially uninterpretable: it does not allow for that 'revenge of the intellect upon art' of which Susan Sontag speaks in her famous essay 'Against Interpretation', which pleads that 'in place of a hermeneutics we need an erotics of art.'[15]

It is this very antithesis between intellectual analysis and immediate response which conditions the effect of art throughout the period we have been considering. Over against the austere and rule-governed (and often enough in paradoxical conjunction with it) there frequently lies an 'erotic' search for the new 'sensory mix'. This is seen in the amazing range of instrumental colourings invented by contemporary composers, and also in that polymorphously perverse breaking down of artistic borderlines which we find in the 'alchemical' transformations of sound in *Hymnen*, the multi-media environment of *HPSCHD*, and other collaged work in which the artistic form is a container for heterogeneous elements. Thus in Berio's *Sinfonia*, we have speech, song, literary texts, dialogue, and political slogans, as well as diverse musical quotations, and in Rauschenberg's collages we may have snapshots, posters, newsprint, comic strips, and so on, all suspended within the pictorial matrix. These mixtures, as we have seen, may defy interpretation—they refuse any clear hierarchic or thematic organization, any neutralizing intellectual dominance on the part of the listener or viewer.

In other works it is bodily sensation itself which actually generates the work of art. The relationship thus forged between creation and effect, however much it may rely upon the inherent drama of inner psychic space, is often wholly impalpable. Imagine, for example, what might be involved in obeying the following instructions from Stockhausen's *For the Seven Days*, which is an example of text– rather than score–inspired 'intuitive' music: 'Play a vibration in the rhythm of your smallest particles; then play a vibration in the rhythm of the universe . . . and of the individual body cells.'[16] The relationship may on the other hand be more direct, as in Mark Boyle's *Son et Lumière for Body Fluids* (1966), which attempted to utilize all possible liquids from our bodies as a source of visual material: in one sequence of this happening, as a couple make love, their electroencephalagrams are projected on to a screen above them. This match between bodily event and 'artistic effect' in another medium is of course no more interpretable than that between bodily movement and sound in John Cage's *Variations V* (1965) in which the movements of dancers trigger off sounds by interrupting light beams.

Nevertheless, such works do offer us a new kind of experience, as they mix sensory modes which had previously been kept separate. (They are thus allied to those works we discussed earlier which crossed conceptual barriers.) Their speed and evanescence and essentially spatial orientation reflect closely the new technology that has made them possible (as in the light shows of progressive pop groups). These considerations apply just as much to more considered and formally organized works, whose result is a permanently available aesthetic object, as to the essentially unrepeatable mixed-media events we have mentioned. One of the earliest and most influential of these works combining different modes was Stockhausen's *Gesang der Jünglinge* (1955–6). This was originally composed in a five-speaker version and is thus one of the first works to exploit stereophonic sound. One result of this was, as Stockhausen notes, that 'the speed of the sound by which one sound jumps from one speaker to another, now becomes as important as pitch once was. And I began to think in intervals of space, just as I think in intervals of pitches or durations. I think in chords of space.'[17] These 'chords of space' can be thought of as having a corresponding basis in 'nature', as when we have a change in pitch as a car passes or a plane flies overhead (indeed the wandering sounds at the beginning of the second region of *Hymen* are very similar to the latter).[18] These correspondences occasionally help us to orient ourselves within electronic music, and yet its sounds are often essentially different in structure from those of conventional music. Indeed, many of the sounds in *Gesang der Jünglinge* are statistically generated so that we cannot look to them for any certainly discernible harmonic figurations: 'I very often use the image of a swarm of bees to describe such a process. You can't say how many bees are in a swarm, but you can see how big or dense the swarm is, and which envelope it has . . . or think of the distribution of the leaves in a tree; you could change the position of all the leaves but it wouldn't change the tree at all.'[19] Thus layer of sound is superimposed upon layer in a complex procedure which gives unpredictable results, not so that one may comment on the other, or even so that they may be separately discriminated, but so that a statistical aggregate of electronic sound is produced. Stockhausen agrees that in traditional music 'the most important principle was that you should always hear everything—every individual tone—so that one wrong note in a chord was immediately noticeable. In statistical compositions, however, the individual components enter into textures which are treated like sounds, but they have an inner life, which is composed.'[20]

This means that for music of this kind the very way in which we listen has to be changed. The sensory order is broken down: the pure electronic sounds may express pitch-relations at one moment and statistical swarms at another; the sung material in this work is also subjected to electronic manipulation to the point at which it is equally 'unnatural', an effect reinforced by its fragmentation into vowel and consonantal components. Stockhausen thus here, as in his later works, demonstrates a kind of metamorphosing equivalence between differing sound sources, as electronic sound approaches melody, and song becomes electronic sound. The text itself, drawn from the Book of Daniel, Chapter Three, evolves from electronically modified sound to syllable, to word, and finally to song. The voice and its message seem to be dehumanized by technological manipulation, so that there is a disturbing tension between the 'natural' discrimination of sound elements and their distortion. This effect is made particularly dramatic by those periodic returns to the normal sensory order, when apprehensible words emerge in melodic sweeps from the six successive types of electronic texture by which Stockhausen has structured this piece. These words prove to be parts of the song of praise by the youths in the burning fiery furnace, particularly 'preiset' or 'lobet' or 'jubelt' in association with 'den (dem) herrn' ('praise the Lord'). The surrounding texture is thus a trial for the emergence of affirmation, though the whole has an inner calmness of development which is far removed from that confrontation between electronic sound and voice which suggests mental breakdown, as in Berio's *Visage*. A work as radically innovatory as this thus poses formal problems for which there are no precedents, and it is difficult to discuss it in any stable critical vocabulary. Indeed this is a problem for electronic music as a whole. A technical description of the means of production can be given, in terms of wave forms, envelope shapes, the function of filters, sequencers, and so on, but there is, as yet, no agreement on the *generic* functions which this complex generating equipment can serve. This is perhaps shown by the fact that the most accessible electronic sound seems to be found in conjunction with more conventional sound sources which *can* set up generic expectations, as in the background of song in *Gesang der Jünglinge* or the commentary of piano and percussion on electronic sound in *Kontakte*. It is difficult too, to give a non-technical description of electronic sounds themselves—we may say for example that their quality in the opening of *Gesang der Jünglinge* is, disregarding the voices, and in quick succession, twittering, burbling like water running out, warbling, tinkling, glassy, echoing, gong-like, humming, xylophone-like, rattling, swishing, liquid, cymbal-like, gurgling, organ-like, plunging, tearing, twittering, skittering, wind-like, surging, organ-like, like glass breaking, and so on, but there is no way of saying how all the elements in this Rabelaisian list manage to combine to make a convincing qualitative progression of types of sound.

As we have already seen, Stockhausen's later 'moment' works like *Kontakte* and *Carré* aim at an even more radical fragmentation and hence at an even greater immediacy of sensory response. To this extent they reflect an attitude to life and an aim which we also find in John Cage: 'living takes place each instant and that instant is always changing. The wisest thing is to open one's ears immediately and hear a sound suddenly before one's thinking has a chance to turn it into something logical, abstract or symbolical.'[21] This is a view that would not have been taken with much seriousness before the 1950s. The fact that so many works like Cage's own *Variations IV* have since been produced according to its prescription marks a profound change in our aesthetic assumptions. This instantaneous and uninterrogated mode of perception is required just as much by those serialist works like *Pli selon pli* whose complexity of organization leads to a perceptual discontinuity, as by those athematic works which concentrate entirely upon texture, by Ligeti and Penderecki. This music requires at one and the same time an acute discrimination between types of sound and a complete passivity with respect to our expectations. Whatever happens it authentically, or at least aesthetically, 'is'. The art we have been discussing is thus in a profound sense imagistic. It abjures those traditional generic forms which secured long-term intelligibility. It cannot move towards reconciliation, climax, or catharsis. The effect of such a mode is to dramatize each moment, and often enough to cause tensions and frustrations which are not to be formally resolved. In this way they may devalue content—sex becomes encephalogram, any sound can be inserted in *Variations IV* without making any difference, urban detritus invades the collage, and texture succeeds texture in *Carré*. The significance of such works thus has to stem to a large extent from our awareness of their technique and our willingness to submit ourselves to their frequently arbitrary results. This produces a constant stimulation and disorientation, but also an emptiness after the psychedelic moment has passed. One can only speculate as to why experience of this kind should be so much valued by avant-garde artists, and upon its significance for the culture in general. The experience overwhelms us, we cannot reduce it to order, and our awareness of its mode of production simultaneously assures us that we need not do so. Such works thus run counter to the whole tradition of art up to the postmodern era, whose most revolutionary and potentially destructive achievement has been this exploitation of indeterminacy and chance. This may reflect the most terrible underlying nihilism, or it may leave us free to react as we will to art in a manner never before possible. Or both.

IV

It is a curious fact already mentioned that much theory-dominated over-determined art has a very similar effect to that we have been discussing. And yet the theory dominated work does seem to guarantee a certain intelligibility, from the critical simplicities masquerading as aesthetic discovery in conceptual art, to the rigorous deductivism of serial music, and the play with language in the new novel. Works of this kind are extreme developments of traditional means; they do not make that historical and conceptual break that we find in extreme kinds of irrationalism and indeterminacy. And yet the difficulties we have in responding to them may be just as great, for their elaborate organization often leads to an overloading effect upon the audience, so that the work may seem as chaotic as other types of work which have deliberately defied mental organization through statistical, aleatoric, paranoiac, or anarchic means—or simple self-contradiction. Thus *Kontakte* and *HPSCHD*, *Projet pour une révolution à New York* and *Nova Express*, are a good deal less far apart in effect than they are in methods of composition.

Thus if one turns from the method of production, the supposed science of 'écriture', to our *response* as we read works in which narrative is distorted or dispensed with, we find that it is at root one of *uncertainty*, rather than that passivity typical of our response to music. This seems to be because it is much more difficult to abolish the lines of narrative cause and effect demanded by the syntax of discourse, than it is to abolish them within the invented and artificial languages of music. In literature we perpetually analyse the 'evidence' and develop hypotheses concerning plot. A radical uncertainty was introduced into this reading process by Beckett, and as we have seen is developed upon rather different aesthetic premises by the new novelists and Burroughs, and also by other experimentalists like Barth, Coover, Brautigan, Barthelme, and Pynchon. Thus in Beckett's *Watt*, the Galls are father and son, or perhaps stepfather and stepson, or perhaps not related at all; and the central symbol of Pynchon's *V* may be Victoria, Vera, Valletta, Vesuvius, Venezuela, or the V made by the receding line of lights in a street, or by spread thighs, or by migratory birds, or the V note where the Whole Sick Crew listen to jazz, or the Venus of Botticelli, or the mons veneris. The narrative method of the Moderns (particularly Faulkner) of course allowed for similar uncertainties, and yet the reader is allowed to have confidence that they can all be resolved within a single spatio-temporal framework. In much post-modern writing such final resolutions are blocked, sometimes jokingly, as in Brautigan's *A Confederate General from Big Sur* (1964) which has five endings, 'Then there are more and more endings; the sixth, the 53rd, the 131st, the 9435th ending, endings going faster and faster, more and more endings, faster and faster until this book is having 186,000 endings per second.'

One of the points of Beckett's writing is that he sees the poignancy of the human effort to resolve uncertainty by imposing an interpretation; and of Robbe-Grillet's, that he really doesn't care about this. Thus Watt and the reader cannot prevent themselves from reflecting upon those incidents of 'great formal brilliance and indeterminable purport' which constitute the novel:

Watt could not accept them for what they perhaps were, the simple games that time plays with space, now with these toys, and now with those, but was obliged, because of his peculiar character, to enquire into what they meant, oh not into what they really meant, his character was not so peculiar as all that, but into what they might be induced to mean, with the help of a little patience, a little ingenuity.[22]

The defeat of such ingenious attempts can perhaps only be fully achieved in the musically unstoppable sequence of the film. Another of Miss Sontag's arguments has its greatest force here, when she says of Robbe-Grillet and Resnais's *L'Année dernière à Marienbad*, that 'the temptation to interpret it should be resisted. What matters . . . is the pure untranslatable immediacy of some of its images.'[23] This echoes in Robbe-Grillet's insistence that 'cet homme, cette femme commencent à exister seulement lorsqu'ils apparaissent sur l'écran pour la première fois, auparavant ils ne sont plus rien; et une fois la projection terminée, ils ne sont plus rien de nouveau'.[24] Thus Robbe-Grillet insists that the mode of existence of his characters is strictly tied to their appearance in the film, and this is reinforced by our feeling that film, like music, is perpetually in the present tense, and thus can cast as much doubt as is needed upon the reality of the past, as happens so effectively in *L'Année dernière à Marienbad*:

Sans doute le cinéma est-il un moyen d'expression prédestiné pour ce genre de récit. La caractéristique essentielle de l'image est sa présence. Alors que la littérature dispose de toute une gamme de temps grammaticaux, qui permet de situer les événements les uns par rapport aux autres, on peut dire que, sur l'image, les verbes sont toujours au présent . . . de toute évidence, ce que l'on voit sur l'écran est en train de se passer, c'est le geste même qu'on nous donne et non pas un rapport sur lui.[25]

These qualities of immediacy, acceptability, and presentness are also implied in Robbe-Grillet's novels, and in the technique of those many writers in France and America whose aims are similar to his own in that they are far more concerned with montage than with historical narrative. They are particularly apparent in the most purely visualizing of the new novelists, Claude Simon, whose work is often explicitly analogous both to film and to the collage procedures of painters like Rauschenberg, whom he admires, and whose aim is to make 'tous les éléments du texte . . . toujours présents' ('all the elements of the text . . . perpetually present') as in a painting (impossible though this is, granted the limitations on human memory).[26]

Simon's *Triptyque* (1973) is explicitly indebted to painting and in particular to Francis Bacon. It is 'une fiction uniquement générée à partir de descriptions' which originally began with two 'scènes' or 'histoires' concerning 'une noce qui tourne mal' ('a wedding which goes wrong') and 'la noyade accidentelle d'un enfant' ('the accidental drowning of a child'), to which a third, 'un fait divers dans une station balnéaire' ('a news item from a seaside resort'), was added to make a triptych after Simon had seen the paintings of that title in the Bacon exhibition in Paris in 1971.[27] These three stories seem to concern, first, some boys out fishing who spy on a couple making love in a barn, thus causing indirectly the death of a child by drowning, secondly, a pair of lovers whose wedding night is spoilt by the drunken husband, and thirdly, an older woman in a hotel bedroom who is asking her wealthy lover to save her son from a drugs charge. Interwoven at intervals there is also a circus scene, which seems to comment on the three stories. All these narrative elements 's'entrelacent, se superposent parfois, se nourissent l'un de l'autre, et finalement, s'effacent'.[28]

One of the chief conventional constraints upon the narrative artist as opposed to the painter has hitherto been that he cannot go back again and again to the same subject, as the painter can, and produce variants. Simon beautifully adapts the techniques of the new novel to make up for this deficiency. For just as the observer's eye is free to move over the canvas, or to compare different versions of the same subject (Cézanne's apples, Monet's haystacks, Bacon's nude studies), to come back again and again to parts, to make new connections, or to perceive new details, so should the writer be free to redescribe with variations and to recombine. Of course we find this in less poetic form in Robbe-Grillet, but Simon goes further; not only do elements of relatively stable series recombine and reveal new aspects, but they may travel, through a series of cinematic dissolves, either exactly or analogously from one scene to another. It is a virtuouso control of 'point of view' in the quite *literal* sense that so distinguishes *Triptyque*. Thus the couple making love in a barn may become part of the design of a poster on its wall, so that through one form of representation another may be perceived. This same 'subject' of the couple making love may thus reappear in a painting, an engraving, a poster, a postcard, or a film which stops and then goes on after a break.[29] Throughout the novel indeed scenes from the three basic stories dissolve into one another across the 'coupures' of the text, as the implied modes of their presentation change. Thus in an engraving on the hotel bedroom wall (which belongs to the third story) we see a metamorphosis into the style of an eighteenth-century picture, of the central incident of the first: a servant girl inside a barn, her legs apart, her raised skirt 'découvrant sa vulve dodue' ('revealing her plump vulva') pushing away without much conviction a 'valet de ferme' ('farm-hand').[30]

Simon thus brilliantly combines visual metamorphosis with that play with language that constitutes 'écriture', and frees it, not of course from narrative as such, but from any dependence upon spatio-temporal continuity, and from that moral significance which arises from seeing characters in a book as continuously 'real' persons. Across the gaps which are so cunningly hidden in the even, present-tense prose of the text, we notice not only the recurrence of scenic motives, but also the purely linguistic permutations of 'écriture'. Simon himself points out that such correspondences between the stories are brought about by 'les métaphores, les tropes, les associations, les oppositions, etc; par exemple, le lapin écorché et la femme nue sur le lit sont tous deux décrits, à quelques pages d'intervalle, en termes exactement semblables'.[31] Such correspondences are even closer elsewhere: thus the rabbit, when hung up by an old woman on a wall, still jerks with 'coups de rein impuissants', and in the next sentence but one, the woman making love in the barn 'accompagne de coups de reins le va-et-vient rythmé'.[32]

This contrast between linguistic patterning and narrative arbitrariness defeats any search for a single underlying narrative unity. For this is a novel, like those discussed earlier, which is 'irréductible à tout schéma réaliste': the relationships we discern between the interlocking series or stories 'ne relèveraient pas d'un quelquonque enchaînement ou déterminisme d'ordre psychologique'.[33] Nor is any part to be privileged above the others, for the mode of narration perpetually makes us aware that 'chacune des scènes n'existerait en tant que texte (affiches, livres, filmes) lu ou vu par les personnages des deux autres'. Their human protagonists are thus deprived of identity and personality. They are always seen as 'personnages' (actors) and frequently as frozen out of emotionally involving activity into some instance of static visual art. They metamorphose themselves into explicitly fictional images.

It is an inescapable fact concerning this mode of writing, that however much it may aim at our acceptance of whatever comes to us in the play of the text, it always nevertheless implies the existence of the rules it is breaking; we are perpetually aware of its deviance from the norms of the past. It is precisely these norms which license my pointing out that all the discontinuous parts of *Triptyque* can be assigned to one of the three stories, or are in the process of moving between them, and that none of these parts is dominant enough to unify the whole. Indeed all the most sophisticated critical techniques of traditional reading are required to aid our appreciation as we trace the metamorphoses and interrelationships of the book's descriptions. Thus a literature consisting *solely* of this mode of writing would be unthinkable; its revolutionary techniques are parasitical upon earlier ones and will remain so, just as analytical cubism will always retain its relationship to representation. The manipulation of the reader largely depends upon a sudden disorientation from realist norms. As Loubère points out, 'sometimes the feeling of reality in *Triptyque* is so strong that the discovery that one is looking at a film or a painting comes as a shock'.[34] The theory of literature thus becomes aesthetically interesting. Its medium and formal procedures become part of its content, as abstraction did of painting. A frequent symptom of this self-consciousness is the '*mise-en-abîme*'; that image in the novel which seems to recapitulate its own procedures. Thus towards the end of *Triptyque* a man in the hotel room completes a jigsaw puzzle, whose image turns out to be the very same hamlet, river, cascade, and so on, of the novel's opening description.[35] The act of assembling the puzzle is analogous to that of reading the novel; the pieces do not correspond with whole objects, any more than do the partial descriptions of the text correspond to completed scenes. And yet this incident almost nostalgically alludes to the reader's desire for that certainty of construction and formal integration and unity of the text which we are, even so, being denied.

In the past, formal procedures seemed to stand in need of some *mimetic* justification; they could, typically, be seen to reinforce some kind of truth. Thus Benjy's and Quentin's temporally confused monologues in *The Sound and the Fury* show that they are trapped in the past; the polysemy of *Finnegans Wake* is partly related to the punning Freud found in dreams; mythological parallels in *The Waste Land* or *Ulysses* articulate double narrative structures which comment on and criticize one another; the fragmented descriptions of objects in the central section of *To the Lighthouse* show the passing of time, and so on. In postmodern literature these procedures are retained with all their virtuosity, but they are there for their own sakes, without their necessarily having any such concomitant mimetic justifications. Thus linguistic correspondences reveal relationships within language itself, and do not necessarily show that the objects they refer to have in themselves any hidden identity or similarity or contrasted mimetic function or significance. The language in which a trout and a phallus are described in *Triptyque* may be noticed to be similar, but there is no concomitant suggestion that these objects have significantly related functions in the real world. The connection here is calculated. The novel guarantees its own intelligibility. But it is an effect of art on the level of 'écriture'. The paradox is that the knowledge of the real world which we need to understand the language in the first place can be so satisfyingly subverted. Thus Simon himself points out that:

> . . . certaines *qualités* communes regroupent ou si l'on préfère cristallisent dans un ensemble des éléments apparement . . . disparates . . . exactement comme certaines qualités communes (harmoniques ou complémentaires, rythme, arabesque) rassemblent dans un tableau, permettent d'y cohabiter en constituant un ensemble *pictorial* cohérent, les objets ou les personnages qui y sont représentés.[36]

It is his brilliant exploitation of these quasi-pictorial conventions that makes Simon's writing the most satisfying within the school of the *nouveau roman*.

V

The technique of the new novel, even if it may defeat the search for an underlying unity, at least allows the reader to have the pleasure of discerning other types of relationship within its play of language. There is in fact a very close correspondence here between compositional method and audience response. The changes in the language of music were not similarly reassuring. Its new language, even when carefully calculated, often failed to depend upon or establish stable generic backgrounds or stylistic procedures which could license that security-conferring series of inferences that we find in literature and much abstract art. Production and consumption failed to correspond, and their mismatch was compounded by enthusiastic critical analyses of composition method which never paused to ask whether the structures they so fanatically dissected were *perceptually* intelligible. In all the excitement of 'Pure Research' the consumability or usefulness of one's product is often conveniently forgotten. It is stratospheric intellectual activity that counts. But after this, what is left? An aesthetic object which should provide us with a certain kind of experience, and this experience, rather than any appreciation of virtuosic notational manipulation, is the ultimate test of its value.

I think we must still maintain that this test is frequently failed by contemporary music on one count: that of the perceptibility of implicative relationships, our sense that music is proceeding in a certain direction. The extreme works like Messiaen's *Modes* and Boulez's *Structures* will never give pleasure in this way. But the fact that such music does provide us with an experience of some kind, and that this does seem to have emotional characteristics, may lead us to defend much postmodern music on another level. The effects I am concerned with can only be appreciated at the price of renunciation—we have not merely to give up a number of critical assumptions, but also to extinguish many old habits of psychological response which are connected with tonal music. However, these renunciations are in essence no more radical than those involved in our giving up representational habits in looking at painting. I will try to make this claim a little more precise.

In our earlier discussion, we assumed that there was a relationship at least in traditional music between signifier and signified, between musical sound and emotional expression, that there was a harmonic syntax and learnt semantics in this sense. (The supporting evidence for this hypothesis has traditionally come from the comparison of the emotional import of music in relation to a verbal text, with similar purely musical procedures in abstract music, and the claim that their emotional effect is at least similar.) We thus, it is asserted, get a sense of music as emotionally expressive, and this sense is tied for most of us to what are perhaps some peculiar physiological facts underlying emotions, those of tension and relaxation. For the harmonic system also can be seen to tense and relax. In the absence of traditional tonality however, what happens? These tensions and relaxations derived from harmonic implication either seem to disappear, or become extremely disorganized, to the point at which one may feel that such music has abjured entirely this quasi-semantic relationship with emotions.

If this is so, then these technical changes will demand an equally radical change in the attitudes of the listener. That is to say, someone who approaches Ligeti, Boulez, Stockhausen, and others, with a 'semantic theory' of emotional expression may be seriously misled. He finds, say, that all atonal music since Schoenberg seems expressionist, anguished, and neurotic—his semantics leads him to believe, for instance, that dissonance 'expresses' psychological tension. In the case of many works of the Second Viennese School he would be absolutely right. But in the case of postmodern music, this would be a hugely over-generalized conclusion to come to, since it is indeed full of dissonance, but clearly is not all intended to inhabit an expressionist emotional world. He would thus be well advised to assume that such music doesn't have a range of emotions to 'express', and may indeed have to give up the notion that it always expresses *specifiable* emotions, of the kind we find in the analysis of music before Schoenberg, any more than abstract painting expresses those specifiable emotions which are associated with real-life objects like peaceful cows or cute kittens or the wrath of God. This is not of course to deny that contemporary experimental music *can* express direct and indeed conventional emotions; on the contrary, one has only to think of the anguish, sadness, and conflict of Henze's *Tristan*, the calm meditation of *Stimmung*, the mystical exaltation of Messiaen, the terrifying mechanical energy of Penderecki's *Symphony* (its opening like a mass of clock and factory machines in conflict), the calm and dreamy slow metamorphoses of sound in Ligeti's *Lontano*, and even perhaps those 'permanent emotions of the Indian aesthetic' which Cage attempts to express in his *Sonatas and Interludes* for prepared piano.

But the problem still remains of the claim to expressivity of a central core of more abstractly organized works, like Lutoslawski's *Preludes and Fugues*, or Maxwell Davies's *Taverner Fantasia* and *Symphony*, or Berio's *Nones*. The last provides a conveniently brief example. It is a serialist work from the fifties. In it we find a whole range of abstract orchestral colourings and relationships, a dynamic range which is not obviously correlated to our tonally derived sense of climax, and so on. The thematic basis (a thirteen-note row) is far removed from that which helped us to correlate earlier music to emotional response and is of course far more difficult to perceive than any traditional theme. And yet work of this type always seems to approach and then cancel a traditional type of expressivity, and what is more, the dissonance/anguish relationship may seem to work here, since *Nones* is related to a poem by Auden concerning Good Friday. But then how can we distinguish such a work from other superficially similar ones (for instance by Nono in the same period) which do not seem to be related to such an underlying emotion?

The listener thus has two sets of problems—of intelligibility and of emotional response. But I do not see that these perplexities, genuinely felt by most listeners, who may be perfectly willing to meet the challenge of works like Beethoven's last quartets or those of Bartok, in themselves invalidate Berio's music. It is just that the usual contrasts of happy/sad, lyrical/agitated, calm/violent and so on, do not apply to much postmodern music in quite the way that they did before. It is hard to imagine a listener who does not find that the Cavatina of Beethoven's Op. 130 is sad; it is easy to imagine a listener who has no idea of the emotion expressed by *Nones*, and who is still moved by the music. Our associations for rhythmic movement are similarly disrupted. Again, on a basically naïve level, we may feel that earlier rhythms may drive along, carry the music, even in Stravinsky's atonal works, and feel by contrast that much postmodern music is 'spasmodic'. And yet, once more, our judgement that the later work is 'spasmodic' may no longer be relevant, once we have been persuaded to stop using earlier music as a standard of judgement. Similarly, the dynamic gestures of contemporary music are so often dislocated from one another, so unrelated to our usual sense of climax, that they cannot be decribed, by the same token, as emotional climaxes.

In sum, in a work like *Nones* we notice contrasts of orchestration, see that they are colourful and varied, that such work is often consistently remarkable for its changing and amazing sounds, but need not expect them to have specifiable emotional correlates any more than abstract painting has them. They are not interpretable in the traditional language, because they are not expressed in the traditional language. We have to accept a presently less intelligible experience, in the hope, no more, that new criteria of value will in the end emerge from it when seen in historical perspective. This does not mean that we do not *hear* Berio, any more than those who failed initially to understand cubism failed to *see* Picasso or Braque. Nor does it mean that on a very subjective level evaluations are impossible. Thus one may value *Nones* for its approaches to traditional power and expressivity more than one does Stockhausen's *Kreuzspiel* for its coolness. What we must not do, is see such works as confused failures to express traditional feelings or relationships, any more than we must judge a Kandinsky, or a Mondrian, or a Pollock, or a Rothko as a confused failure to express the feelings aroused by representational painting. Like painting indeed much new music has become abstract in a wholly new sense, and the pains and travails of adjustment are just as great as they were for abstract painting long ago. Indeed they are greater in the case of music, because the work of Schoenberg and his colleagues has been so long in gaining acceptance. Just as Picasso moved further and further away from the representational portrait, and succeeded in producing an abstract cubist structure, so music has given up its traditional emotional physiognomy (and physiology), and our emotional response, which may be a very deep one, as it can be to abstract painting, has to be allowed to have a different basis.

VI

This need to learn a new language, which involves also a willingness to allow the work of art to be apparently more abstract, less committed to the external world and to the emotions and beliefs which we entertain in it, seems to be one of the common denominators of much of the work we have looked at in this essay. Our close attention to abstract design, to immediate sense experience, to 'écriture', to purely abstract combinations of sound divorced from traditional expressivity, all involve our seeing art as *form*. It was this aspect of avant-garde activity that led me to argue earlier that we have in our age a new aestheticism.

But a final caveat has to be entered against my own argument. It is inevitable in trying to approach original art, to try to tackle first such formal problems, which are unique to it. Thus much of the modernist achievement was equally seen to have involved the stylization and formalization of aspects of external reality—in cubism, in narrative manipulation in the novel and poetry, in the concentration on the image and symbol rather than the philosophically discursive, in rhythmic and melodic fragmentation, and the impressionistic handling of the orchestra, and so on. Nevertheless, in the perspective of time just such mimetic conventions have become apparent for modernist works. Thus, with pop painting behind us, we may become more sensitive to the urban realism of the great cubists—their use of commerical imagery—posters, newspapers, and print. Similar mimetic commitments will no doubt soon become apparent for the postmodern era. Whether the world they prove to articulate will be a tolerable one remains to be seen.

*   *   *

There are no simple conclusions to be drawn from the preceding essay; no single key to the *Zeitgeist*, no single dominant technical procedure, no single type of response demanded of us. Any intellectual tidying-up of this kind would merely add to the simplifications and overgeneralizations that are inevitably to be found in a treatment as cursory as this has been. I am thus forced to conclude with a number of distressingly obvious pieties for which the foregoing will have to be the evidence, and obvious though they are, they seem to me to be of considerable importance, or I would not have written this book. Thus the post-war years gave birth to a period of artistic achievement quite distinct from that of modernism. We already know that we have a number of major works of painting, music, and literature that are definitive of our age—exactly how, we are uncertain. These works, once we have overcome some of the obstacles to understanding that I have tried to indicate above, are, some of them, still extremely frustrating and wholly trivial. But others have a profundity, a complexity, and a power, that will I will imagine ensure that they endure. The challenge to us, their contemporaries, is to learn their new languages, so that we may begin to get to know them, not simply for the satisfactions they offer, but so that we may meet the greatest of challenges to those concerned for the arts: that of inhabiting the present rather than taking refuge in the past.

Notes

Chapter One

1. Michel Zeraffa, 'The Novel as Literary Form and as Social Institution' in E. Burns and T. Burns (eds.), *The Sociology of Literature and Drama* (Harmondsworth, 1973), 53.
2. Cf. Stephen Heath, *The Nouveau Roman* (London, 1972), 25–9.
3. Albert Camus, *Le Mythe de Sisyphe* (Paris, 1956), 130. 'In this universe the work of art is then the sole opportunity to maintain one's consciousness and to fix its adventures. To create is to live twice.'
4. For example, in K.L. Goodwin, *The Influence of Ezra Pound* (London, 1966).
5. Robert Lowell, 'Thomas, Bishop and Williams', in *Sewanee Review*, lv (1947), 503.
6. Robert Lowell, 'William Carlos Williams', in Charles Tomlinson (ed.), *William Carlos Williams* (Harmondsworth, 1972), 372.
7. Cf. Christopher Butler, 'Robert Lowell: from *Notebook* to *The Dolphin*', *Yearbook of English Studies*, viii, (1978), 141–56.
8. Randall Jarrell, in Tomlinson, op. cit., 174.
9. Jean Paul Sartre, *La Nausée* (ed. Folio, Paris, 1973), 61–2. 'This is what I have been thinking: for the most commonplace event to become an adventure, you must—and this is all that is necessary—start *recounting* it. This is what fools people: a man is always a teller of tales, he lives surrounded by his stories and the stories of others, he sees everything that happens to him through them; and he tries to live his life as if he were recounting it. But you have to chose: to live or recount.' (Trans. Robert Baldick, Harmondsworth, 1965)
10. Michel Butor, *La Modification* (ed. 10/18, Paris, 1970), 283. 'You hear the shouts of porters, the shrilling of whistles, the puffing and creaking sounds of the other trains.

    You stand up, put on your coat, take your case and pick up your book.

    The best thing, surely, would be to preserve the actual geographical relationship between these two cities,

    and to try to bring to life in the form of literature this crucial episode in your experience, the movement that went on in your mind while your body was being transferred from one station to another through all the intermediate landscapes.

    towards this book, this future, necessary book of which you're holding in your hand the outward form.

    The corridor is empty. You look at the crowd of people on the platform. You go out of the compartment.' (Trans. Jean Stewart, London, 1958)
11. John Cage, cit. Richard Kostelanetz, *John Cage* (London, 1974), 11.
12. Pierre Boulez, *Par volonté et par hasard: entretiens avec Célestin Deliège* (Paris, 1975), 34, 44. 'strong, expanding civilisations have no memory: they reject, they forget the past . . . once history has been liquid-

ated, one has only to think of oneself.' (Trans. *Eulenberg*, London, 1976)

13. This is the title of an article by Boulez in *The Score*, 6 (May 1952), 18–22.

14. Donald Judd, in Gregory Battcock (ed.), *Minimal Art* (New York, 1968), 150.

15. Ibid. 155.

16. Robert Sherlaw Johnson, *Messiaen* (London, 1975), 62.

17. Karlheinz Stockhausen, in Jonathan Cott, *Stockhausen: conversations with the composer* (London, 1974), 35.

18. Alain Robbe-Grillet, in an interview in *Revue de Paris* (January 1959), 134. 'my style is nearer to that of dodecaphonic music, based upon a series of twelve tones, than to tonal music.'

19. Robbe-Grillet, *Pour un nouveau roman* (Paris, 1963), 35. 'To tell a story well, then, is to make what you write resemble the prefabricated synopses that people are used to: in other words, to make it resemble their ready-made idea of reality'. (Trans. Barbara Wright, London, 1965)

20. Ibid., 36. 'even to the point where invention and imagination may finally become the subject of the book' (Trans. Barbara Wright)

21. Ibid., 38. 'contain a "plot" of the most easily discernible kind . . . the movement of the writing is more important in them than that of the emotions and the crimes.' (Trans. Barbara Wright)

22. Bruce Morrissette is a favourite target, for example in Heath, op. cit. 120 f.

23. Robbe-Grillet in an interview in *Le Figaro Littéraire* 1 September 1962, 9.

24. Gérard Genette, *Figures I* (Paris, 1966), 85. 'Put another way, it spreads out horizontally, within a spatio-temporal continuity, the vertical relationship which unifies the diverse variations upon a theme, it sets out in a series the terms involved in a choice, it transposes concurrence into concatenation.'

25. Robbe-Grillet, *Pour un nouveau roman*, 12. 'After *Les Faux-Monnayeurs*, after Joyce, after *La Nausée*, it seems as though we are making our way more and more towards an epoch in fiction in which the problems of writing will be seen clearly by the novelist, and in which critical concerns, far from sterilizing creation, will be able on the contrary to serve it as a motive force.' (Trans. Barbara Wright) The first chapter of Jean Ricardou's *Pour une théorie du nouveau roman* (Paris, 1971) is significantly entitled 'La littérature comme critique'.

26. Cf. Irving Sandler, *Abstract Expressionism: the triumph of American painting* (London, 1970), 30.

27. In their 'Letter to the Editor', *New York Times*, 13 June 1943. (Section 2, page 9.)

28. Jackson Pollock, in answer to a questionnaire printed in *Arts and Architecture*, 2 (February 1944), 14.

29. Cf. Sandler, op. cit. 107–8.

30. Cf. B.H. Friedman, *Jackson Pollock* (New York, 1972), 40 ff.
31. *Life*, 11 October 1948. The remarks quoted were made by Sir Leigh Ashton, Aldous Huxley, Theodore Greene, and A. Hyatt Major (curator of prints at the Metropolitan museum) respectively.
32. Jackson Pollock, in F.V. O'Connor, *Jackson Pollock* (Museum of Modern Art, New York, 1967), 80.
33. Harold Rosenberg, 'The American Action Painters', in his *The Tradition of the New* (reprinted, London, 1970), 36.
34. Jackson Pollock, in the *New Yorker*, 5 August 1950, 16.
35. Robert Motherwell, in an interview with Max Kozloff, *Art Forum*, iv, 1 (September 1965), 37.
36. Hilton Kramer, cit. Maurice Tuchman, *The New York School* (London, n.d.), 204, from 'The end of modern painting', *The Reporter*, xxi, 2, (23 July 1959), 41 f.
37. Cf. Sandler, op. cit. 270 ff., and for a more amusing point of view Tom Wolfe, *The Painted Word* (New York, 1978).

Chapter Two: I

1. Igor Stravinsky, in Robert Craft (ed.), *Conversations with Igor Stravinsky* (Harmondsworth, 1962), 144.
2. Susan Sontag, *Against Interpretation* (London, 1967), 100.
3. Pierre Boulez, cit. Joan Peyser, *Boulez* (London, 1977), 20.
4. George Perle, *Serial Composition and Atonality* (2nd ed., London, 1963), 2.
5. Cf. Leonard E. Meyer, *Music, the Arts and Ideas* (Chicago, 1967), 240.
6. Paul Jacobs, liner notes to his Nonesuch recording of *Modes*, on H 71334.
7. Pierre Boulez, *Par volonté et par hasard*, 70.
8. Cf. György Ligeti, 'Pierre Boulez', *Die Reihe*, iv (Bryn Mawr, Philadelphia, 1961), 36–62, and Reginald Smith Brindle, *The New Music* (London, 1975), 25–33.
9. Boulez, op. cit. 70. 'For me it was an experiment in what one might call Cartesian doubt, to bring everything into question again, make a clear sweep of one's heritage, and start all over again from scratch, to see how it might be possible to reconstitute a way of writing that began with something which eliminates personal invention.' (Trans. *Eulenberg*)
10. Boulez, op. cit. 72.
11. Boulez, op. cit. 65. 'For me this represents a very special procedure: this accumulation that springs from a very simple principle, to end in a chaotic situation because it is engendered by material that turns in on itself and becomes so complex that it loses its individual shape and becomes part of a vast chaos.' (Trans. *Eulenberg*)
12. Boulez, op. cit. 27.

13. Boulez, op. cit. 28. 'Whether it be a book, a picture or a piece of music, these polyvalent levels of interpretation are fundamental to my conception of the work.' (Trans. *Eulenberg*)
14. Ligeti, op. cit. cited in Meyer, op. cit. 211 f.
15. In Jonathan Cott, *Stockhausen: conversations with the composer*, 220 f.
16. Cott, ibid. 223.
17. Hans Keller, 'Music 1975', *New Review*, ii, 24 (March 1976), *passim*.
18. George Rochberg, 'Indeterminacy in the New Music', *The Score*, 26 (January 1960), 11 f.
19. Olivier Messiaen, in Claude Samuel, *Entretiens avec Olivier Messiaen* (Paris, 1967), 48. 'Some of my later works also include note rows, but they haven't anything like the sound one would expect to find in a serial development, nor have they the "serial spirit"; they remain coloured because, fired by my love for colour, I treat them as colours.' (Trans. Felix Aprahamian, London, 1976)
20. Cf. Robert Sherlaw Johnson, *Messiaen*, 92 f.
21. Cf. Meyer, op. cit. 246.
22. Johnson's analysis of *Chronochromie* is of particular interest, op. cit. 159 ff.
23. Olivier Messiaen, in Samuel, op. cit. 154.
24. Smith Brindle, op. cit. 53.

Chapter Two: II

25. Paul Valéry, *Œuvres Complètes I* (Paris, 1957), 1300 f. 'Poets go deliberately into the enchanted forest of language in order to lose themselves, and to intoxicate themselves with their own bewilderment, in looking for the crossroads of significance, unforeseen echoes, and strange encounters. They fear neither detours, nor surprises, nor darkness; but the huntsman who urges himself on to track down the truth, to follow a single and continuous path, whose every part shall be the only one he can take in order not to lose the trail or the road already covered, runs the risk of capturing nothing in the end but his own shadow. Gigantic sometimes, but a shadow all the same.'
26. Henry James, 'The Future of the Novel' (1899), in Morris Shapira (ed.), *Henry James: selected literary criticism* (Harmondsworth, 1968), 218.
27. Jorge Luis Borges, *Labyrinths* (Harmondsworth, 1970), 51.
28. Ibid. 53
29. The work of Jean Ricardou (*Problèmes du nouveau roman* (Paris, 1967); *Pour une théorie du nouveau roman* (Paris, 1971)), and of critics in colloquia organized by him, for example that which resulted in *Nouveau roman: hier, aujourd'hui* (2 vols, Paris, 1972), and which was succeeded by colloquia on Robbe-Grillet and Claude Simon, will amply confirm this judgement.
30. Roland Barthes, *Essais critiques* (Paris, 1964), 164. 'Thus realism cannot be the copying of things, but must be the knowledge of lan-

guage; the most "realistic" work will not be that which "paints" reality but that which explores as profoundly as possible the unreal reality of language.'

31. Philippe Sollers, 'Écriture et révolution', *Tel Quel: Théorie d'ensemble* (Paris, 1968). 'that which has been called "literature" belongs to a finished epoch, which is giving way to a nascent science, that of writing.'
32. Claude Simon, 'Débat sur le roman', *Les Nouvelles Littéraires*, 22 June 1961, 7.
33. Claude Simon, *Orion aveugle* (Geneva, 1970), 6.
34. Tzvetan Todorov, *Poétique* (Paris, 1968), 20. 'the particular text only serves as an example which allows description of the properties of literature'.
35. Cf. Stephen Heath, *The Nouveau Roman*, 25–9, and his 'Ambiviolences', *Tel Quel*, 50 (1972), 22–43, and 51 (1972), 64–76.
36. Jacques Derrida, Introduction To E. Husserl, *L'Origine de la géomètre* (Paris, 1962), 105; cit. Heath, op. cit. 25. (Joyce's writing) 'no longer translates from one language into another on the basis of commonly accepted meanings, but flows through all languages at one and the same time. It accumulates their energies, actualizes their most hidden consonances, reveals their most distant of common horizons, cultivates associative syntheses instead of fleeing from them, and restores the poetic value of passivity.'
37. Cf. John Sturrock, *The French New Novel* (London, 1969), 160 ff.
38. John Fletcher, *New Directions in Literature* (London, 1968), 113.
39. Cf. Robbe-Grillet's many interventions in the colloquia on the nouveau roman, op. cit.
40. Robbe-Grillet, in *Nouveau Roman: hier, aujourd'hui I*, op. cit. 127.
41. This statement of Robbe-Grillet and those which follow come from the *prière d'insérer* distributed with *Projet pour une révolution à New York* (Paris, 1970). They were taken from an article in *Le Nouvel Observateur* of 26 June 1970. 'From now on it is indeed the themes of the novel themselves (objects, events, words, formal movements, etc.) which become the basic elements engendering all the architecture of the story (récit) and even the adventures which unfurl within it; this is according to a mode of development comparable to that employed by serial music or modern art and sculpture.'

'Far from disappearing, the anecdote thus sets about growing; discontinuous, plural, mobile, subject to chance, pointing out its own fictitiousness, it becomes a "game" in the strongest sense of the word.'

'I take them quite freely so far as I am concerned, from the mythological material which surrounds me in my daily life.'

'various things . . . shop windows . . . posters'.

'When I walk through the corridors of the subway, I find that I am assailed by a multitude of signs which, taken as a whole, make up the mythology of the world I live in, something like the collective unconscious of society; that is to say, at one and the same time the image it wishes to give out of itself, and the mirror of the troubles which haunt it.'

'Shown up in the light of day as stereotypes, these images cease to function as snares from the moment when they are taken up by a living discourse, which remains the only space for my freedom. I know now that this city which oppressed me is imaginary; and in refusing to submit in alienation to its constraints, its fears, its ghosts I wish on the contrary to reinvest them with my own imagination.'

42. Cf. John Weightman, *The Concept of the Avant-garde* (London, 1973), 316 f.

43. 'The Baby Sitter' is one of the short stories in Robert Coover's collection *Pricksongs and Descants* (London, 1971).

44. Robbe-Grillet, *Projet*, 141–3. 'After having sniffed the still liquid blood, several trickles of which varying in length have run across the tiles, and glanced in all directions, the rat now grows bolder: it sits up on its hind legs and hesitantly moves its forelegs and its snout over the body of the victim lying on her back in an abandoned, limp position, her charms preferred rather than concealed by the torn and bloodstained shreds of the long white nightgown. The animal, which seems particularly attracted by the wounds of the seven daggers thrust into the tender flesh at the top of the thighs and the lower part of the belly, all around the sticky pubic hair, the hairy animal is so large that, while still keeping its hind legs on the floor, it nonetheless manages to explore the fragile lacerated skin from the anus to the area around the navel where the bare flesh reappears, still intact here, in a broad, fraying rip of the thin linen material. It is here that the rat decides to sink its teeth, and begins devouring the belly.' (Trans. Richard Howard, London, 1973.) Other later encounters with the rat occur on 149 f. and 195 f.

45. Cf. the curious dialogue concerning the method of narration of *Projet* on 188 ff.

46. Robbe-Grillet, in *Nouveau Roman: hier, aujourd'hui I*, 97. 'You cannot claim that I play in order to escape the tragic, since, on the contrary, the game denounces the tragic as being a human creation, which another human creation can destroy.'

47. Ibid. 127. 'The serious attitude presupposes that there is something behind our gestures: a soul, a god, values, the bourgeois order . . . whereas behind the game there is nothing . . . the game affirms itself as purely gratuitous.'

48. *Prière d'insérer*, for *Projet*. 'After the bankruptcy of the divine order (of bourgeois society) and after that, of rational order (of bureaucratic socialism) it must now be understood that only lucid organizations remain possible. Revolution itself is a game as the most aware of the May revolutionaries used to say.'

49. Robbe-Grillet, *Pour un nouveau roman*, 21. 'But the world is neither meaningful nor absurd, it quite simply *is* . . . all around us defying our

pack of animistic or domesticating adjectives things *are there*. Their surface is smooth, clean and intact without false glamour, without transparency. The whole of our literature has not yet managed even to begin to penetrate them, to alter their slightest curve.' (Trans. Barbara Wright)

50. Ibid. 13, 15. Robbe-Grillet's early work is interestingly discussed from this point of view in Bernard Bergonzi, *The Situation of the Novel* (Harmondsworth, 1972), 46 f., and in Patrick Swinden, *Unofficial Selves* (London, 1973), 83 ff.

51. Cf. Harold Rosenberg, *Art on the Edge* (London, 1976), 278, 44.

52. Barnett Newman, cit. Maurice Tuchman, *The New York School*, 112.

53. Thomas B. Hess, *Barnett Newman* (Tate Gallery, London, 1972), 24. Hess prints the complete typescript essay by Newman, 20 ff.

54. Ibid. 24.

55. Cit. Hess, ibid. 50.

56. Ibid. 34.

57. Ibid. 36.

58. Barnett Newman, 'The ideographic picture' (Betty Parsons Gallery, New York), 20 January–8 February 1947; cit. Tuchman, op. cit. 105.

59. As seen in the exhibitions, 'Towards a New Abstraction' at the Jewish Museum New York in 1963, and 'Post Painterly Abstraction' at the Los Angeles County Museum in 1964.

60. Lawrence Alloway, in Gregory Battcock (ed.), *Minimal Art*, 39.

61. Frank Stella, in Battcock, ibid. 157 f.

62. Robert Rosenblum cites Rubin in his *Frank Stella* (Harmondsworth, 1971), 18.

63. Frank Stella, Pratt Institute Lecture (1959–60), printed in Rosenblum, op. cit. 57.

64. Rosenblum, op. cit. 48.

65. Most particularly, Michael Fried, 'Art and Objecthood', *Artforum*, June 1967, reprinted in Battcock, op. cit. 116 ff.

66. Suzi Gablik, *Progress in Art* (1977), 45 f.

67. Ibid. 87.

68. Sam Hunter's observation may be relevant here: 'The boredom of rudimentary forms, lacking much visual interest, or of standardised compositional elements from which manual evidence of distinctive authorship has been eliminated, also tests the "commitment" of the art audience at a time when there is too much facile appreciation of culture' (*American Art of the Twentieth Century* (1970), 312). But has culture ever been too facilely appreciated, and if it had, would not minimal art precisely encourage this 'facility'?

69. Carl André, in Andrea Gould, 'Dialogues with Carl André', *Arts*, May 1964, 27.

70. The Jewish Museum, New York, 'Primary structures: young American and British sculptors', 27 April–12 June 1966.

71. Carl André, cit. David Bourdon, in Battcock, op. cit. 104.

72. Ibid. 107.

73. Diane Waldman, Introduction to *Carl André* (Guggenheim Museum, New York, 1970).
74. Sol LeWitt, 'Paragraphs on Conceptual Art' in Alicia Legg (ed.), *Sol LeWitt* (Museum of Modern Art, New York, 1978), 166.
75. Sol LeWitt, 'Incomplete Open Cubes', John Weber Gallery, New York, 26 October–20 November 1974; subsequently shown in Oslo, Edinburgh, Turin, Basel, Cologne, Eindhoven, Geneva, Oxford, and Amsterdam. The art magazine and the travelling exhibition establish an artist's right to a style.
76. Mel Bochner, 'Serial Art, System, Solipsism' in Battcock, op. cit. 101.
77. This influence is noted by Bernice Rose, 'Sol LeWitt and Drawing' in Legg, op. cit. 34.
78. Sol LeWitt, 'Paragraphs', op. cit. 166.
79. Sol LeWitt, cited from conversation by Lucy Lippard in Legg, op. cit. 24.
80. In Legg, op. cit. 33.
81. Robert Rosenblum draws this analogy in Legg. op. cit. 18.
82. Bob Law, Catalogue statement, *Ten Black Paintings*, Museum of Modern Art, Oxford, 21 May–23 June, 1974.
83. These are reproduced in Ursula Meyer (ed.), *Conceptual Art* (New York, 1972), 196 f., as are a number of the works described above and below.

Chapter Three: I

1. Cf. Wilfrid Mellers, *Caliban Reborn* (London, 1968), 99.
2. Claude Samuel, *Entretiens avec Olivier Messiaen*, 39. 'For me certain sonorities are linked with certain complexes of colour and I use them as colours, juxtaposing them and putting them in relief against one another, as a painter underlines one colour with its complementary.' (Trans. Felix Aprahamian)
3. Translated from the preface to the score of *Couleurs de la cité céleste* (Leduc, Paris, 1966), 'Première note de l'auteur'.
4. Igor Stravinsky, in Robert Craft (ed.), *Conversations with Igor Stravinsky*, 121.
5. Pierre Boulez, *Par volonté et par hasard: entretiens avec Célestin Deliège*, 86.
6. Ibid. 88 f. 'If one introduces into a structure of fairly simple rhythms accumulations of grace notes that cause the tempo to be interrupted the whole time, one completely loses the idea of speed.' (Trans. *Eulenberg*)
7. Ibid. 89.
8. Igor Stravinsky, in Craft, op. cit. 141, 142.
9. Hans Keller, 'Music 1975', *The New Review*, ii, 24 (March 1976), 37.
10. Desmond Shawe-Taylor, the *Sunday Times*, 31 August 1975, 23.
11. Pierre Boulez, op. cit. 122, 123. 'What attracted me in Mallarmé . . . was the extraordinary formal density of his poems . . . never has the

French language been taken so far in the matter of syntax.' (Trans. *Eulenberg*)

12. Karlheinz Stockhausen, cit. Karl H. Worner, *Stockhausen: life and work* (London, 1973), 46 f. Worner reprints a number of Stockhausen's programme notes, from which I quote here and below.
13. Ibid. 43.
14. Robin Maconie, *The Works of Karlheinz Stockhausen* (Oxford, 1976), 124.
15. Stockhausen, sleeve note to the recording of *Stimmung* on DG 2543-003.
16. In Jonathan Cott, *Stockhausen: conversations with the composer*, 149.
17. George Devine, in a programme note to the National Theatre production of *Play* in London, 7 April 1964.
18. Samuel Beckett, *Watt* (New York, 1959), 74. (First published in Paris in 1953.)
19. Samuel Beckett, 'Three Dialogues with George Duthuit', in *Transition Forty-Nine*, 5 (December, 1949), 97–103; reprinted in Martin Esslin (ed.), *Samuel Beckett* (Englewood Cliffs, N.J., 1965), 17.
20. Samuel Beckett, *The Unnameable, Three Novels by Samuel Beckett* (New York, 1965), 314.
21. Samuel Beckett, *Comment c'est* (Paris, 1961), 9. 'how it was I quote before Pim with Pim after Pim how it is three parts I say it as I hear it' Samuel Beckett's English version, published as *How It Is* (London, 1964).
22. Ibid. 21. 'the sack when it's empty my sack a possession this word faintly hissing brief word and finally apposition anomaly anomaly a sack here my sack when it's empty bah I've lashings of time centuries of time.' (Trans. Beckett)
23. Ibid. 85. 'table of basic stimuli one sing nails in armpit two speak blade in arse three stop thump on skull four louder pestle on kidney five softer index in anus six bravo clap athwart arse seven lousy same as three eight encore same as one or two as may be'. (Trans. Beckett)
24. Ibid. 146. 'and these same couples that eternally form and form again all along this immense circuit that's the millionth time that's conceivable as the inconceivable first and always two strangers uniting in the interests of torment'. (Trans. Beckett)
25. Ibid. 53. 'I'm often happy God knows but never more than at this instant never so oh I know happiness unhappiness I know I know but there's no harm mentioning it'. (Trans. Beckett)
26. Cf. ibid. 74, 139.
27. Ibid. 174. 'if all that yes if all that is not how shall I say no answer if all that is not false yes

all these calculations yes explanations yes the whole story from beginning to end yes completely false yes'. (Trans. Beckett)
28. Jean-Paul Sartre, Preface to Natalie Sarraute's *Portrait d'un inconnu* (Paris, 1948), 7 f. 'Antinovels preserve the appearance and the con-

tours of the novel . . . But that is in order to deceive [or: disappoint] the better; it is a matter of making the novel fall into dispute with itself, of destroying it beneath our eyes at the same time as one seems to be building it up.'

Chapter Three: II

29. Jonathan Raban, *The Society of the Poem* (London, 1971), 44 f.
30. Michel Butor, *Mobile* (Paris, 1962), 131. 'The most important religious practice of the Europeans in America is their pilgrimage to the sacred city of Washington, where the principal temples and the essential organs of government are found.'
31. Cf. Roland Barthes's review of *Mobile*, reprinted as 'Littérature et discontinu' in his *Essais critiques* (Paris, 1964), 175–8.
32. Robert Rauschenberg, 'Note on Painting Oct. 31– Nov. 2, 1963', in John Russell and Suzi Gablik, *Pop Art Redefined* (London, 1969), 101.
33. Lawrence Alloway, *Figurative Art Since 1945* (London, 1971), 202.
34. Robert Rauschenberg, 'Random Order', *Location*, 1 (1963), 26 f.
35. Michael Crichton, *Jasper Johns* (London, 1977), 34.
36. Richard Hamilton, cit. Richard Morphet, *Richard Hamilton* (Tate Gallery, London, 1970), 30.
37. Richard Hamilton, *Architectural Design*, 10 (October 1962), 485–6. Reprinted in Russell and Gablik, op. cit.
38. Ibid.
39. Ibid.
40. Luciano Berio, liner notes to his recording of *Sinfonia* on CBS Classics 61079.
41. Stockhausen, in Jonathan Cott, *Stockhausen: conversations with the composer*, 130 f.
42. Ibid. 136.
43. Eric Saltzman, in Richard Kostelanetz (ed.), *John Cage*, 150.
44. John Cage, *Silence* (London, 1973), 10.
45. In Cott, op. cit. 174.

Chapter Three: III

46. Daniel Spoerri, in the catalogue to his exhibition at the Centre National des Arts Contemporains, Paris, 1972.
47. William Burroughs, 'The Cut Up Method of Brion Gysin', *Yugen*, 8 (New York, 1962), unpaginated.
48. William Burroughs, *Nova Express* (London, 1964), 180.
49. Ibid. 84.
50. Ibid. 56.
51. Ibid. 103.
52. Ibid. 68.
53. Ibid. 11.
54. William Burroughs, *Snack* (London, 1975), unpaginated.

55. Burroughs, *Nova Express*, 106.
56. Karl H. Worner, *Stockhausen: life and work*, 39.
57. John Cage, *Silence*, 59.
58. Henry Cowell, in Richard Kostelanetz, *John Cage*, 97.
59. Kostelanetz, ibid. 174 f.

Chapter Four

1. Cf. John Cage, *Silence*, 10.
2. Albert Camus, *Le Mythe de Sisyphe*, 134.
3. Andy Warhol, cit. John Russell and Suzi Gablik, *Pop Art Redefined*, 117.
4. My account here follows Ruby Cohn, *Back to Beckett* (London, 1973), 265.
5. Clement Greenberg, in Bernard Smith (ed.), *Concerning Contemporary Art* (Oxford, Clarendon Press, 1975), 11.
6. Clement Greenberg, 'Avant Garde Art and Kitsch', *Art and Culture* (Boston, 1965), 10.
7. Lawrence Alloway, 'The Arts and the Mass Media', *Architectural Design* (February 1958).
8. Harold Rosenberg, *The De-Definition of Art* (London, 1972), 218.
9. Donald Barthelme, *Snow White* (New York, 1967), 13.
10. Ibid. 16.
11. Ibid. 132.
12. Ibid. 141.
13. Ibid. 139.
14. Ibid. 106.
15. Donald Barthelme, 'After Joyce', *Location, 1* (Summer 1964), 15.
16. George Maciunas, cit. Michael Nyman, *Experimental Music: Cage and beyond* (London, 1974), 66 f.
17. Cit. Nyman, ibid. 112.
18. Daniel Bell, *The Cultural Contradictions of Capitalism* (New York, 1976), 20.
19. John Weightman, *The Concept of the Avant-garde*, 29.
20. Harold Rosenberg gives an extremely penetrating account of this episode in his *Art on the Edge*, 285 ff.
21. This is one example among many of this mode of thinking, to be found in Jean Ricardou (ed.), *Claude Simon* (Paris, 1975), 263 f.
22. Jeffrey L. Sammons gives a devastating analysis of this type of fallacy in his *Literary Sociology and Practical Criticism* (London, 1977), 16–39.
23. Leo Steinberg describes his reactions to these works (by Johns and Rauschenberg) in his *Other Criteria* (London, 1972), 15, 22.
24. Stockhausen's pretensions in this respect are attacked by Leonard Meyer, *Music, the Arts and Ideas*, 78fn, 254.
25. Clement Greenberg, 'Modernist Painting', *Arts Yearbook, 4* (New York, 1961), 101–8.
26. Tom Wolfe, *The Painted Word*.

27. Cf. Steinberg, op. cit. 79.
28. Rosenberg, *The De-Definition of Art*, 129.
29. Patrick Heron, in Bernard Smith (ed.), op. cit. 164 f.
30. Mary Ellen Solt, *Concrete Poetry: a World View* (London, 1970), 6.
31. John Barth, *Lost in the Funhouse* (Harmondsworth, 1972), 109.
32. Richard Poirier, *Mailer* (London, 1972), 123. He is referring, unfairly I think, to Borges.
33. These stories appear in Robert Coover's collection *Pricksongs and Descants*.

Chapter Five

1. Michael Nyman, *Experimental Music: Cage and beyond*, 3.
2. Andy Warhol, in an interview with Gerard Malanga, *Arts Magazine*, xli, 4, 1967.
3. Marcel Duchamp, cit. Edward Lucie-Smith, *Movements in Art since 1945* (1975), 11.
4. Jasper Johns, cit. Michael Crichton, *Jasper Johns*, 43.
5. Claus Oldenburg, in John Russell and Suzi Gablik, *Pop Art Redefined*. 96.
6. Adolf Gottlieb, cit. Maurice Tuchman, *The New York School*, 71.
7. Francis Bacon, in David Sylvester, *Interviews with Francis Bacon* (London, 1975), 60.
8. Harold Rosenberg, *Art on the Edge*, 67.
9. Mondrian's methods are interestingly discussed from this point of view in C.H. Waddington, *Beyond Appearances* (Edinburgh, 1969), 39–44.
10. Frank Stella, in Gregory Battcock (ed.), *Minimal Art*, 149.
11. Robert Morris, 'Notes on Sculpture II', *Artforum*, v (October 1966), 23.
12. Morris Shapiro, cit. Tuchman, op. cit. 20.
13. Robert Rosenblum, *Modern Painting and the Northern Romantic Tradition* (London, 1975), 214.
14. Mark Rothko, in Seldon Rodman, *Conversations with Artists* (New York, 1957), 93 f.
15. Susan Sontag, *Against Interpretation*, 14.
16. Karlheinz Stockhausen, in Jonathan Cott, *Stockhausen: conversations with the composer*, 39.
17. Stockhausen, in Cott, ibid. 87.
18. Ibid. 110, 91.
19. Ibid. 68.
20. Ibid. 70.
21. John Cage, cit. Nyman, op. cit. 1.
22. Samuel Beckett, *Watt* (London, 1963), 71 f.
23. Susan Sontag, op. cit. 9.
24. Alain Robbe-Grillet, *Pour un nouveau roman*, 165. 'The man and woman don't start to exist until they appear on the screen for the first time;

before then they were nothing, and the moment the film is over they are again nothing.' (Trans. Barbara Wright)

25. Alain Robbe-Grillet, *L'Année dernière à Marienbad* (Paris, 1961), 15. 'No doubt the cinema is the pre-ordained means of expression for a story of this kind. The essential character of the image is its present-ness. Whereas literature has a whole gamut of grammatical tenses which makes it possible to narrate events in relation to each other, one might say that on the screen verbs are always in the present tense . . . by its nature what one sees on the screen *is in the act of happening*, we are given the gesture itself, not an account of it.' (Trans. Barbara Wright)
26. Claude Simon, in *Nouveau roman: hier, aujourd'hui, II* (Paris, 1972), 89.
27. Claude Simon, in Jean Ricardou (ed.) *Claude Simon* (Paris, 1975), 410.
28. *Prière d'insérer* to Claude Simon, *Triptyque* (Paris, 1973). They 'interweave, superimpose themselves on one another sometimes, feed off one another, and finally, fade out'. (Trans. H.R. Lane, London, 1977)
29. Cf. Claude Simon, *Triptyque*, 195–7.
30. Ibid. 42–3.
31. Claude Simon, in *Claude Simon*, 425. 'metaphors, tropes, associations, oppositions, etc.; for example the flayed rabbit and the naked woman on a bed are both described, a few pages apart, in exactly similar terms.'
32. Claude Simon, *Triptyque*, 25. 'jerking its haunches helplessly' . . . 'accompanies with jerks of the hips the rhythmic back and forth motion'. (In this translation by H.R. Lane the repetition implicit in 'coups de reins' is lost.)
33. Claude Simon, in *Claude Simon*, 424. 'irreducible to any realistic schema' . . . 'cannot be referred back to any linking or determinism of a psychological kind'.
34. J.A.F. Loubère, *The Novels of Claude Simon* (Cornell, 1975), 221.
35. Claude Simon, *Triptyque*, 220 ff.
36. Claude Simon, in *Nouveau Roman: hier, aujourd'hui II*, 80 f. 'certain common qualities group themselves, or if one prefers, crystallize, within an ensemble of apparently . . . disparate . . . elements, exactly as certain common qualities (harmonic or complementary, rhythm, arabesque) come together in a picture, and allow the objects and characters which are represented there to cohabit within a coherent pictorial ensemble.'

The translations are by the author, unless otherwise attributed.

Index of Names